Teaching Writing in the Content Areas:

COLLEGE LEVEL

The Author

Stephen N. Tchudi, past president of the National Council of Teachers of English, is Professor of English and of American Thought and Language at Michigan State University, East Lansing. He is also the coauthor of *Teaching Writing in the Content Areas: Elementary School, Teaching Writing in the Content Areas: Middle School/Junior High,* and *Teaching Writing in the Content Areas: Senior High School,* published by NEA, and the creator of the NEA In-Service Training Program *Writing in the Content Areas.*

The Advisory Panel

Libby G. Cohen, Associate Professor of Special Education, University of Southern Maine, Gorham

Irene Duprey-Gutierrez, English and Journalism Instructor, Newbury College, New Bedford, Massachusetts

Neill Megaw, Professor of English (retired), University of Texas at Austin

Eula Ewing Monroe, Professor of Teacher Education, Western Kentucky University, Bowling Green

Kevin J. Swick, Professor of Education, College of Education, University of South Carolina, Columbia

John W. Taylor, Associate Professor of English and Linguistics, and Director of Composition, South Dakota State University, Brookings

Daria Portray Winter, Instructor, Department of English, University of the District of Columbia, Washington

Teaching Writing in the Content Areas:

COLLEGE LEVEL

Stephen N. Tchudi

Note

The opinions expressed in this publication should not be construed as representing the policy or position of the National Education Association. Materials published as part of the Writing in the Content Areas series are intended to be discussion documents for teachers who are concerned with specialized interests of the profession.

Library of Congress Cataloging in Publication Data

Tchudi, Stephen, 1942–
    Teaching writing in the content areas.

    Bibliography: p.
    1. English language—Rhetoric—Study and teaching.
2. Interdisciplinary approach in education.   I. National
Education Association of the United States.   II. Title.
PE1404.T36 1986   808'.042'0711   86–712
ISBN 0-8106-0786-7

ju
10-30-8?

Contents

Preface

During the past decade, two phrases have captured the interest of college instructors concerned about the quality of their students' writing: *writing in the content areas* and *writing across the curriculum*. This monograph discusses both topics.

Writing in the content areas refers to the pedagogical possibility that writing can be taught through subject-matter courses as well as in English classes and that students can deepen their knowledge and understanding of a discipline by writing about it. The philosophy of *writing in the content areas* holds that every faculty member should consider him/herself a teacher of writing. While this notion has obvious appeal for English faculty, it has received wide support from instructors in areas as diverse as science, fine arts, applied arts, social science, humanities, and mathematics.

Writing across the curriculum is a related concept which implies that faculty coordination of teaching writing must be a collegewide concern. This monograph, then, maintains the distinction that "writing in the content areas" generally refers to what individual instructors do with writing in their own classes, while "writing across the curriculum" describes attempts to organize writing in entire academic units.

The book begins with the area of smaller, but more important, focus: the individual instructor in the individual classroom. Chapters 1 through 5 present a "rhetoric" or "primer" of content-area writing, assuming that college instructors will want to know something of the theory and research that underlie various practices, but stressing a good many practical teaching ideas. Also included are a summary of recent investigations into the role of writing as a means of learning and numerous examples of writing in various disciplines.

Chapters 6 and 7 explore faculty involvement in writing-across-the-curriculum programs. Chapter 6 features five narratives prepared especially for this publication by colleagues who have introduced writing programs of various kinds on their campuses. Chapter 7 provides a series of "lesson plans" for faculty workshops to encourage readers to move from the printed page to action. An extensive bibliography is also included to help faculty groups conduct further research on their own.

I want to thank a number of colleagues and friends who assisted me in preparing this monograph. I am especially grateful to the five people who contributed narratives for Chapter 6:

Patrick L. Courts, State University of New York at Fredonia
Margaret Parish, University of North Carolina at Wilmington
Patricia L. Stock, The University of Michigan
Mark L. Waldo, Montana State University
Art Young, Michigan Technological University.

In addition, the members of the Advisory Panel, whose names are listed on page 2, provided insightful comments and criticisms.

I also want to thank colleagues in business, mathematics, science, technical service, and English at Delta College, University Center, Michigan, who served as field testers of the final array of faculty workshops presented in Chapter 7. Their responses and reactions were especially helpful.

1. Writing in the Content Areas: An Overview

On July 9, 1892, the National Education Association established a Committee on Secondary School Studies made up of both school and college educators. The Committee's charge was to explore college admissions requirements and examine each subject commonly taught as preparation for college. It was to

> consider the proper limits of [that] subject, the best methods of instruction, the most desirable allotment of time for the subject, and the best methods of testing the pupils' attainment therein . . . (72, p.3)*

This "Committee of Ten" was chaired by Harvard's President, Charles W. Eliot, who had earned a reputation for reform with his emphasis on teaching "modern" subjects—science, English, mathematics, and the modern foreign languages.

At the time, the nation's secondary schools were under enormous criticism for a variety of perceived faults. College educators, led by the Harvard faculty, had been especially critical of entering freshmen's preparation in written composition (57, 54). Both scholarly and popular articles by Harvard faculty had complained about poor English teaching and called for dramatic improvement of composition instruction in the schools. Not surprisingly, the Committee of Ten recommended four years of compulsory high school English, including a strong component of rhetoric and composition.

The Committee also saw an opportunity for language instruction through the disciplines:

> There can be no more appropriate moment for a brief lesson in expression than the moment when the pupil has something which he is trying to express. If this principle is not regarded, a recitation in history or in botany, for example, may easily undo all that a set exercise in English has accomplished. (72, p. 87)

Members of the English faculty may balk at a phrase like "a set exercise in English," for we know, to borrow from John Dixon (21), that language is "best learnt in actual operation, not through dum-

---

*Numbers in parentheses appearing in the text refer to the Bibliography beginning on page 122.

my runs." However, the Committee of Ten had grasped the crucial idea that language is most effectively learned when it is being used to accomplish a genuine purpose.

Unfortunately, the Committee was more concerned with correctness of spelling and usage than with substance of thought. Thus it was calling for a kind of "correctness across the curriculum," rather than what we know as *composing* in the content areas.

As Joanne Yates has shown in her NEA monograph, *Research Implications for Writing in the Content Areas* (105), only after the progressive education movement, led by John Dewey, were students (and their language) given an active role in learning. Under progressivism, language was seen as an outgrowth of creative intellectual activity, not just a proper record of it. She reports that many schools and colleges of the 1920s, 1930s, and early 1940s developed interdisciplinary, project-oriented curricula, many of them centering on language activity.

The high point of the progressive interest in content writing can be seen in *A Correlated Curriculum*, prepared by a committee of the National Council of Teachers of English under Ruth Mary Weeks (101). This far-sighted document called for teachers to make connections among schools subjects, for "failure to correlate the various subjects of instruction leaves the student unaware of their connection as related parts of a scheme of life" (101, p. 1).

One committee member, F. Earl Ward of Macalester College, proposed linking English and history through literature in the freshman and sophomore years and "research projects, individual and socialized," in the upper levels and graduate school:

> Papers written in such courses should be accorded an audience wherever possible. If publication is not practicable, reading before a group of students with like interests and problems should be planned, or the papers should be filed where they will be available. (101, p. 83)

Another committee member, Julian Drachman of Morris High School, New York City, called for college-level integration of science and English through "instruction in exposition, the study of models of scientific literature, and practice in original science writing." He reported that this "new type of course has been in existence for some years in the universities of Columbia [New York] and elsewhere" (101, pp. 42–43). Morris was not concerned with the teaching of what we might call "technical writing," but with integrating language study with a sociocultural outlook on science. "At the University of Chicago," he noted, "this plan takes the

10

form of a series of general survey courses in one of which—a survey of the natural sciences—training in both reading and writing is given" (101, p. 43).

Many ideas proposed in the *Correlated Curriculum* were indeed close to current views of writing across the curriculum. The correlation movement never gained a great deal of momentum, however, and most of its recommendations were not implemented in many schools or colleges. In several respects, the proposals were ahead of their time, especially in the notion of "fusion" of disciplines into interdisciplinary study. Even today one finds very few examples of truly interdisciplinary work where disciplinary barriers have been dissolved. Some literacy proposals of the correlated curriculum were undoubtedly lost in the larger problem of course fusion.

Perhaps even more fatal to the correlated curriculum was World War II, when English teachers turned their attention to patriotic literature and schools became training grounds for the war effort rather than centers of interdisciplinary inquiry. When the war ended, there was little evidence of anything resembling writing across the curriculum in American schools and colleges, except in the occasional technical or business writing course.

In the late 1940s and in the 1950s and 1960s, however, one does find a persistent complaint about the quality of writing done by school and college students. In the 1950s, for example, Navy Admiral Hyman Rickover, an outspoken critic of the alleged softness of American education, accused it of producing illiterates. His sentiments were echoed by Rudolph Flesch, whose *Why Johnny Can't Read* attacked what he perceived as the pernicious influence of progressivism. And when the Russian Sputnik went into orbit, the media described a crisis in education of major proportions, including frequent worries about writing and reading skills.

In retrospect, the early 1960s—the post-Sputnik years—might have been ripe for the introduction of content-area writing in schools and colleges. Given the strong interest in technical education, the meshing of writing with subject-matter instruction would have been natural. Yet there was no strong push to connect writing instruction with the disciplines, only an occasional attempt to do something along those lines. (Northwestern University, for example, briefly experimented with freshman writing courses taught in the academic departments, but concluding that little or no writing was done, dropped the experiment.)

For more than three quarters of a century, then, there have been continuing concerns about the quality of school and college writing, along with periodic recognition of the potential of writing in the disciplines to provide a solution. In actual practice, little has changed. Composition at the college level has remained the domain of the English department.

Several recurring issues and problems explain the failure of writing in the content areas to catch on. First, many college English faculty have shown themselves uneager to teach composition. This lack of interest has not gone unnoticed by colleagues. The English department aversion to writing can be traced back to the late nineteenth century, when Harvard's English faculty articulated the prevailing view that composition instruction was essentially the domain of the secondary schools. Harvard lamented that its instructors had to spend time grading themes when they could be doing other things (presumably teaching upper-level literature and language courses). To its credit, Harvard did have a serious writing program, including English A, the grandparent of all freshman composition courses. Still, the Harvard instructors thought the theme work was beneath them, and their attitude has been reflected by college English departments ever since.

In the 1960s, some colleges dropped required freshman composition altogether, a move curiously inconsistent with the post-Sputnik concerns about literacy skills. The commonly offered argument was that college students were writing better than ever (SAT verbal scores were at an all-time high). However, senior faculty at these institutions often privately confessed that the department was weary of teaching composition classes.

At the present time, basic writing courses are often taught by graduate assistants or part-time faculty. Although full professors of English occasionally teach writing (in some colleges it is a matter of department policy that all senior faculty teach some writing), it is nonetheless evident that writing is not something especially valued by English departments. Having failed to devote full energies to writing, English departments do not sound persuasive when they call for writing taught across the curriculum.

Second, few college teachers have felt particularly knowledgeable about teaching writing. Despite the fact that writing is a major activity for many scholars, few have had training in writing beyond the freshman level. Ironically, many English faculty share this insecurity and lack of experience; they have been trained to teach literary scholarship, not writing. Further, until quite recently, good research in writing instruction has been scarce. Thus college faculty have either taught writing as it was taught to them as freshmen or have developed idiosyncratic approaches. Composition has been something taught by intuition or foggy memory, and few college professors have felt comfortable doing that.

Third, and perhaps most important, is that subject-matter professors have simply been too busy covering their own syllabi to take on writing. Aside from the general suspicion that writing in the content areas is an English department trick to foist off responsibility for writing, content faculty have seen no way to squeeze significant amounts of writing into their courses (especially if that writing creates stacks of papers to correct).

As I write in the mid-1980s, however, some things have happened to heighten the interest among college teachers in writing. All over the country faculties from various disciplines are meeting to discuss composition programs in the disciplines, and many (although by no means a majority of) subject-matter professors are not only finding time to include more writing in their courses, but are offering testimonials to its success and usefulness.

I trace these changes in attitude and practice to two publishing events, initially unrelated, in 1975.

On December 8, 1975, *Newsweek* magazine published a cover story with a modified title borrowed from Rudolf Flesch: "Why Can't Johnny Write?" The article began, "Willy nilly the educational system is spawning a generation of semiliterates" (74). The root of *Newsweek's* interest in literacy could be unearthed in the announcement by Educational Testing Service (ETS) that scores in the Scholastic Aptitude Test verbal section had declined 40 points in the previous decade. Why? *Newsweek* wondered. It found the answer in what it saw as loss of structure and discipline in the schools, leading to a decline in writing instruction. The *Newsweek* report caught the attention of the general public (including university faculty members) and suddenly this nation added a "writing crisis" to its list of problems.

In fact, *Newsweek's* analysis contained a number of serious flaws. In the first place, ETS had pointed out that the decline in test scores was no absolute measure of literacy. The SAT is, after all, an aptitude test, not an achievement test. Later research revealed that the bulk of the decline could be traced to the changing college-going population. American colleges and universities had grown enormously during the 1960s and early 1970s, particularly through affirmative action programs. A new generation of students was being offered the opportunity for two- or four-year college education; it was predictable that a more broadly representative college population would produce, on the average, lower test scores.

Reflecting on the pervasive notion of a decline in literacy, Robert Pattison of Long Island University has remarked:

13

To convince me that today's graduate is less literate, you would have to show me that his capacity to use language in dealing with the world was less than his forebear's. You would have to show me that what he had lost in reading and writing was not compensated by a gain elsewhere in his linguistic makeup. And you would have to show me that his use of language was less well adapted to survival in this world than the literacy of his predecessor was to survival in the world of fifty years ago. (77)

Five years after the *Newsweek* article appeared, a good deal of evidence suggested to me that despite genuine worries over the quality of student writing, there was little reason to suppose that today's college students are significantly less literate than those of previous generations (54).

Nevertheless, as Laurence Behrens of American University has observed, whether writing skills have declined absolutely, "What's certain is that students today are *widely believed* to be more illiterate . . . " (5, p. 54). In a 1978 study of faculty colleagues, he reported that 41 percent felt that writing skills had declined "to some extent"; another 37 percent felt skills had declined to "a great extent"; and only 3 percent saw any improvement in their students' writing abilities. The problems most frequently identified by Behrens's respondents were usage, spelling, and punctuation (67 percent); writing quality (65 percent); vagueness (57 percent); insufficient evidence or research (50 percent); disorganization (48 percent); incorrect diction (48 percent); poor quality of thought or logic (46 percent); dullness (43 percent); incoherence (31 percent); and incorrect format (20 percent) (5, p. 55).

That spelling and mechanics should head the list is not surprising; those surface features are most obvious to readers, and such errors are a red-flag indicator of alleged "illiteracy" to a great many people. Interestingly, however, a number of the problems identified by the American University faculty are essentially problems of content and thinking: insufficient evidence, poor quality of logic, incoherence. This survey too, then, has implications for content-area writing instruction.

My own historical studies into the teaching of English (54, 55) suggest that the problems perceived by Behrens's colleagues were not unique to the 1970s; they are perennial concerns that accompany a pervasive notion that students of any era are less literate than those of yesteryear. In the 1890s, when the Harvard faculty was concerned about a perceived decline in writing, students had the same general problems of correctness and coherence. In 1890 as in

1978, college students floundered about with academic writing and did a poor job of polishing their papers into standard written English.

Nevertheless, the net effect of the *Newsweek* article was to stimulate interest in writing. For perhaps the first time in the history of higher education, writing and writing theory have been recognized as crucial components of the college curriculum. Jobs for Ph.D.s in English are scarce, but the job placement list of the Modern Language Association shows opportunities for composition specialists. Further, there has been a blossoming of high-quality writing research. Where 20 years ago writing instruction was rather a mystery, today some well-established principles of writing instruction exist, supported by a growing body of research.

Much of that research has grown up as a reflection of the second significant publishing event of 1975: James Britton's *The Development of Writing Abilities (11-18)* (11). In this book, Britton and his colleagues at the University of London Institute of Education reported their research on the uses of writing in London city schools. They found that when done at all, writing generally served perfunctory examination functions, not true communication. The writing to "teacher as examiner" was wooden and dull.

Drawing on the psychological work of Jean Piaget and L. S. Vygotsky, Britton articulated the concept of *language as a way of knowing*. Language, he said, is not a passive tool for transcribing knowledge; it is inextricably bound up with learning itself. One cannot separate knowing from languaging. The very act of writing, Britton argued, forces a person to reconsider and reorder his or her thinking. Britton recommended that school writing be expanded, with writing used to help students learn in disciplines across the curriculum.

Janet Emig of Rutgers University argued similarly that higher cognitive functions "seem to develop most fully only with the support of verbal language" (29, p. 123). She specifically advanced the notion that writing is a unique mode of learning because it involves three patterns: *enactive* (learning by doing), *iconic* (learning through images), and *symbolic* (learning through representations). Writing thus involves hand, eye, and brain.

Steven Zemelman has argued that writing

> is not a separate skill students acquire before learning other subjects; rather, it is a complex process combining many mental activities, each depending on and influencing the others: enumerating, categorizing, developing terms, gaining a sense of active participation in a subject,

15

sensing and analyzing one's reactions to a situation, abstracting, seeing new connections and underlying patterns, developing arguments, developing hierarchies of significance. (106, p. 228)

Other writers have elaborated that argument and shown how it applies in such disciplines and fields as mathematics (53), philosophy (88), science (61, 100, 19), physics (57), foreign languages (91), English as a second language (89), economics (42), business (31), and media study (65). "Writing in the right setting," Zemelman concluded, "is not just communication of what one already knows, but is central to the act of learning" (106, p. 229).

The link of writing to learning opens the door to programs in content-area writing that may be more successful and widespread than those of the past. Where in 1892 the Committee of Ten saw writing as proper expression of thought, and in 1936 the Correlated Curriculum Committee saw it as a service to the disciplines, the newer theory pledges something even better for content teachers: *improved learning*.

The claim in the 1980s is not simply that content teachers ought to include writing in their disciplines in order to teach writing, but that they should use it as a means to improve education. Put baldly, proponents of content writing agree that papers written in the disciplines will result in students knowing more and knowing better than they do without writing. The student who writes a variety of essays will know more about the discipline than the one who merely answers multiple-guess tests. The student who maintains a journal or learning log will learn more than the one who fills in blanks in a laboratory workbook. The student who struggles with ideas in history, philosophy, art, mathematics, music, psychology, philosophy, or literature through essays will have a deeper understanding than the one who merely writes down notes on lectures and recites them in a quiz section or on a short answer exam.

John Stevenson (90) claims that "writing is a liberal art." It helps develop broad faculties of critical thinking and perceiving. The college student who writes in the content fields will not only be a better writer, but a better thinker, a more liberally educated man or woman.

It would be useful and dramatic at this point to introduce a research study providing conclusive support for these claims, something showing a direct and positive correlation between, say, the amount of writing done in a college curriculum and achievement tests or grade point averages. Unfortunately, no such study has been completed, and it is doubtful that such clear and decisive evidence will ever be found. Writing is still too much art and not enough science, too much bound up with living and learning, for that to happen.

Nevertheless, the literature contains testimonials about the value of content writing in science (10), health and physical education (70), social studies (7), and journalism (35).

Other research studies have explored parts of the writing/knowing relationship. Van Nostrand (96), for example, found that when students were given fragmentary bits of knowledge and asked to synthesize them in writing, 85 percent "incorporated new information beyond the first stated principle of relationship," so that writing induced synthesis of present and past learning. Newell (73) found that essay writing in a social studies class promoted integration of ideas from prose reading.

Newell's study also showed that research in this field is not always predictable. It did not show the expected gains when writing was linked to two other tasks: notetaking and generalizing. His conclusions were complicated, however, by the fact that he was having students do fairly conventional school writing tasks, rather than having them write according to currently accepted principles. In other words, he found that ordinary copy-it-down writing led to little improvement in knowing.

Not just any writing, then, will produce improved learning *or* writing. Indeed, Knolblauch and Brannon (60) have worried that many of the "new" writing-across-the-curriculum programs are merely "grammar across the curriculum" or "packaging information across the curriculum" with a focus on "formal shells" of writing, rather than substance. Such programs are not likely to produce perceptible changes in learning. "Writing enables new knowledge," they explain, only when it involves that "active effort to state relationships which is at the heart of learning" (60, pp. 467–68).

The best and most satisfactory test of the effectiveness of content writing is both simple and complex: Try it and see how you like it.

This monograph is dedicated to helping content teachers see ways of incorporating writing in their classes successfully and in keeping with current writing theory. Part of the discussion deals with the topic of assessment and evaluation. This not only includes the issue of theme marking, it also emphasizes seeing how well writing does, in fact, enhance learning. The "final examination" that follows reading of the monograph is for content instructors to assign some writing, assess it carefully, and determine for themselves whether the claims of writing in the content area seem valid.

2. Writing and Learning— "Workaday" Writing

"Rhetoric" is a term that is widely used and seldom defined. Most commonly it has come to mean fraudulent or deceptive use of language—the "rhetoric" of politicans and hucksters. In the more specialized world of the writing instructor, it simply refers to the principles that govern the creation and assessment of discourse. Rhetoric is the study of writing (and speech), with a distinguished history that goes back to Aristotle and Plato. Because classical rhetoric, especially under Aristotle, was concerned with "invention," or the generation of material for speech, its domain has, in some respects, been all of human knowledge. At its worst, rhetoric has been concerned with dressing up ideas in language that will assuage or gull a reader/listener. At its best, rhetoric seeks to articulate the relationships among the substance of discourse, the ways in which that substance is generated or discovered, and the means by which writers and speakers go about shaping their ideas and understandings for an audience.

One hundred years ago, rhetorics written for college courses spoke comfortably of the "laws" of discourse, which were seen as more or less identical to the laws of mind. And until quite recently, college writing classes were dominated by a nineteenth century tradition with professors articulating the characteristics and patterns of writing, and students required to create facsimiles (58). The nineteenth century rhetorics and their twentieth century clones—the freshman comp handbooks—were *prescriptive*, based on the assumption that the simplest way to create a writer was to teach the inviolable laws of rhetoric and mind.

In the past two dacades, rhetorics and views of writing and mind have changed. Writing teachers are now a good deal less cavalier about setting forth rules and laws. Good rhetoric books are now *descriptive*, offering a broad picture of writing and writers, rather than prescriptive.

Further, writing instructors have come to realize that the "laws" of rhetoric are, in fact, much more flexible and complex than some of our predecessors had imagined. Here it is useful to borrow a metaphor from Michael Polanyi, who, in *Personal Knowledge* (80), likens knowing in any subject to the knowledge of a bicyclist. A bike rider, he explains, can articulate broad principles of riding: one climbs on the bike, pedals, steers, and balances. Scientists can elaborate on that knowledge, and through study of slow motion films, they can describe the cycling process in fine detail. Yet there remains only one good way to teach a child to ride a bike: place him or her on the seat, give a few instructions, get the child started, and then let go. Polanyi explains that the internalized knowledge of the cyclist far exceeds the formal knowledge that we can articulate.

Writing is a bit like riding a bicycle (including the adage that once you know how to do it, you never forget, but you may grow rusty). Although writing is governed by some general principles, and those principles can be articulated in rhetoric books and by writing teachers, the writer—even if relatively inexperienced—often knows more subtle behaviors than can be taught. Many unskilled writers, in fact, get into trouble, not because they do not know "the rules," but because they follow the rules slavishly, rather than relying on their intuitive knowledge and ability to figure things out. They are novice cyclists trying to learn while reading a physics treatise on bicycling.

James Britton, previously cited as a founder of the content-writing movement, has explained that most writers come to internalize rules through practice (12). These rules are discovered "by modes which are indistinguishable from the modes in which those rules were . . . generated in the first place" (p. 73). He explains that "rules" or "principles" or "conventions" come about, after all, because they serve to simplify or clarify communication. Rhetorical rules are constantly being renegotiated as people master them through trial and error and employ them with others.

From this understanding of the nature of rules comes the central pedagogical premise of the "new" approach to writing:

Writing is a learn-by-doing skill.

At first glance, that precept may seem simplistic. On close examination, however, it implies a complex pedagogy. Strictly speaking, bicycling is a learn-by-doing skill, but few people have learned to cycle without support, coaching, and encouragement. (Indeed, a person utterly unfamiliar with a bike who was given one might never figure out its use.) Writing, like cycling, is learned by doing with modeling, critical suggestions, and an occasional good hard push.

Although some content instructors have doubts about their ability to do the right kind of coaching, in fact, much of what they should

19

do will come intuitively if they follow the single rhetorical precept of this chapter:

Keep content at the center of the writing process.

By that I simply mean that if instructors in the disciplines will focus on the learning that takes place through their students' writing, many of the writing skills will take care of themselves. The content teacher of writing need not buy a freshman composition handbook or a grammar text and pore over it because of a 30-year time lapse between taking writing and teaching it. The strengths that content teachers bring to writing are knowledge of their discipline, of its intricacies and curiosities, its procedures, its growth and development, its particular uses of language. By keeping attention clearly focused on content and giving students plenty of learn-by-doing practice, the instructor in the discipline can effectively teach writing.

One of the simplest ways to focus on content, enhance learning, and supply writing practice is through what I have come to call "workaday" writing.

PERSONALIZING KNOWLEDGE THROUGH WRITING

"Workaday" writing has three broad characteristics that make it a good way to initiate writing in the content areas:

1. It is generally short and impromptu, not requiring large amounts of student or class time.
2. It is written primarily for the benefit of the writer as an aid to clarifying experience; thus,
3. It does not require extensive instructor commentary and response (theme correcting).

D. L. Pearce of Eastern Montana University has observed that "Writing on a topic being covered in class requires students to examine the concepts and facts involved, to focus on and internalize important concepts, and to make those concepts at least to some degree their own" (78, pp. 212–13). Pearce also recognizes that, in practice, much writing done in college classes is of a routine sort that has students record information rather than "internalize knowledge." The writing/learning often follows what C. W. Griffin has labeled the "prove-approve" model, where the student proves knowledge through writing and the instructor approves the finished product (43). Although writing can cometimes be very helpful for

20

purposes of record keeping, Griffin argues—borrowing from Bloom's *Taxonomy of Educational Objectives*—that students should write to *understand, remember, highlight, apply, analyze*, and *synthesize*.

Linda Flower of Carnegie-Mellon University has suggested that students can enhance their personal knowledge of disciplines through what she has labeled "writer-based" prose, "a verbal expression written by a writer to himself and for himself" (34, p. 21). Such writing is

> the record and working of his own verbal thought. . . . [It] reflects the associative, narrative path of the writer's own confrontation with her subject . . . (34, p. 21)

Because of its personal nature, writer-based prose does not work well for published writing; in fact, it will often fail to make connections with an audience beyond an immediate circle of fellow learners. A serious problem in teaching writing is that many novice writers can create only writer-based prose and need instruction and help with audience awareness. Rather than dismissing writer-based prose as something on the lower rungs of a hierarchy of composition, however, Flower sees it as essential not only in planning formal (or reader-based) writing, but in helping students engage with their studies. She thus encourages students to generate quantities of it in response to their class work.

I prefer to use the term "workaday" writing to describe the general kind of writing under discussion here. It is functional, practical—workaday—because it grows directly from students' need to get things done in class or laboratory. By consciously thinking of its value, most content instructors can multiply the amount of writing in their classes manyfold by introducing workaday writing activities systematically, almost daily.

THE FORMS OF WORKADAY WRITING

Notetaking

I once heard a speaker describe how he has his students throw away their notebooks on the first day of class. He dramatically requires them to dump their spiral-bounds in the wastebasket and explains that he wants them to *learn* in this course, not scribble down facts. I take the speaker's point but think that a form of workaday writing would work even better for him.

I teach my students what I call "personalized notetaking" (92). Instead of copying down facts from texts or lectures, students

21

should interact constantly with their material—critically, analytically, aesthetically, *personally*. Their notes should reflect their point of view as well as the content of a course. (My students report that this kind of notetaking also helps them stay awake over pedantic texts or in slow lectures; they can entertain themselves with their own writing.)

I suggest that they ask themselves questions: "What do you think of this material? What amazes you? What did you know already? What puzzles you? What makes you angry?" (Yes, content often makes people angry, especially when it conflicts with common sense or commonly held beliefs.)

I have my students analyze the thinking pattern of a lecturer or a textbook writer, a task of informal rhetorical analysis that helps them see that content is often delivered by another human being, someone with individual biases and prejudices: "Where did this writer get the facts? Are there any ideas here that you question? Could this have been written from a different perspective? Does the professor always reduce information to the same pattern, and if so, does this tell you something about him/her or the discipline?"

Personalized notes need not be read or evaluated by the instructor, although I usually collect the notebooks from time to time to see if students have the basic ideas. Personalized notes are generally a private piece of writer-based prose, however—an aid to the student in mastering the field (but providing a fringe benefit to everyone by increasing the amount of learn-by-doing writing being produced).

Journals

Toby Fulwiler of the University of Vermont is a strong advocate of "journals across the disciplines" (36). A journal is more formal than a set of notes; if focuses on students' *reactions* to readings or lectures or discussions rather than emphasizing content. Journal keeping is extraordinarily popular in school and college English courses, and the chances are good that content instructors will find their students familiar with the idea.

Customarily students are asked to write in their journals several times a week—a page or two or three each time. Sometimes the journal writing is done at the beginning of class hour; often it is done outside class at the students' choice of times. Students can go over past learnings, raise issues and problems that confuse them, and write full responses to their learning. Generally instructors "prime the pump" for journal writing by supplying lists of ideas for writing, but the choice of subject is left to the student.

Many instructors find journals a valuable preparation for class discussion. A five-minute journal write at the beginning of the hour helps many students participate more fully in class discussions. Journals can also be used for reactions to texts and lectures, to outside reading, and as a place to make connections between the course and the real world or between the course and others in the department or college.

Although essentially writer-based, journals should also communicate with the instructor, who collects them from time to time for reading and response. I tell my students that I will not respond to every item in their journals (a task that would obviously be impossible with classes of any but seminar size). Rather, I scan the journals for highlights and to get a sense of the interaction with the course material that is taking place. I also invite students to star or asterisk items to which they particularly want a response from me.

Responding to journals is emphatically *not* theme grading or marking. Because the journals are writer-based, there is no point in focusing on matters of spelling, punctuation, and usage. (I insist that journals be legible, and I encourage students not to be sloppy in matters of usage; but I do not analyze for or mark down errors.) My response to journals is personal and informal. I react to statements that catch my eye, raise questions, supply answers. I find that responding to journals is a pleasure rather than a chore, and it helps me get to know my students better.

For the content teacher, response to the journal can focus on the central rhetorical precept of this chapter:

Keep content at the center.

If the instructor's response focuses on the course material (rather than on qualities of writing), the writing will take care of itself. Is the student getting the material? Can his/her understandings be clarified or deepened? Are there any points in the course that the student has missed?

In only one sense should the content instructor attend to writing quality: vague, murky, incoherent, jumbled prose may be an indication that the student is missing course content. The writing quality is thus a reflection of content mastery.

In large lecture classes, responding to journals may be impossible for the instructor (and/or the teaching assistant). A useful alternative procedure is to advise students at the beginning of the class that the journal is semipublic. The instructor can then set aside a few minutes from time to time for students to read what they regard as their most interesting/angry/unusual entry to a pair or trio of peers sitting in the same section. Or students may tear out a significant entry and pass it forward for anonymous reading by the instructor and public response.

Journals in the disciplines are generally not graded. There is no easy way for an instructor to assess a journal as an "A" or a "C." Rather, journals are often put on a pass/fail or credit/no credit basis as a part of the broad course requirements.

Free Writings

Stephen Marcus of the University of California, Santa Barbara, has developed variations on another kind of workaday writing, the "free" writing. In this kind of activity, students write free associations to whatever comes into their minds in response to a reading, lecture, or discussion (66). To provide focus for writing, Marcus uses the following assignments (here presented in a paraphrase):

- Write down three words that were important in today's assignment and explain their importance.
- Do a three- to five-minute free write on the topic of today's class as a warmup for discussion.
- Respond to a "seed sentence." (Here the instructor chalks a key concept or provocative sentence on the board.)
- Prepare for laboratory by writing down what is to be done in lab, any confusion as to procedures, and what this experiment is expected to create or prove.
- Do a "postwrite," summing up or reacting to a lecture, discussion, chapter, or laboratory experience.

Once again, such writings are made an integral part of the class and do not require instructor response. Although the free writes may be collected from time to time, if the instructor wishes to monitor student thinking, they are essentially "self-assessing," since they lead directly into class activities.

Microthemes

These "mini-essays," as described by the faculty at the University of North Carolina at Wilmington (95), are short writings that can be typed or handwritten on 5- × 8-inch note cards. They can be scanned quickly by professor or teaching assistant for key points, or they can be evaluated by peers in small groups. The UNCW faculty uses the themes for five purposes: *summaries, writing and support-*

ing a thesis, posing questions, working with class data, and *providing support for generalizations.* In Chapter 6, Mark Waldo of Montana State University describes a similar activity, illustrated by an economics professor who has developed some 60 topics for microthemes used in his classes.

OTHER WORKADAY FORMS

Figure 1 provides a list of other workaday writing forms. This figure also contains space for content instructors to add forms specific to their disciplines. To find those forms, instructors may need to look no further than their desks. The various notes and memos that pile up in the course of work are precisely the stuff of which workaday assignments can grow.

Most workaday writing is, as I have observed, writer-based. As a term progresses, however, content instructors may want to encourage students to make this writing more and more reader-based, first using it to clarify concepts, then to share information productively with others. Some possibilities follow.

Reading Reports

Often students will do individualized reading outside class. Their learnings can be pulled together in a report, abstract, summary, or précis to be shared with other students. Such writing may aim for pure objectivity, but the instructor may want such reports to reflect the writer's own responses and reactions. A good report may strike a spark with peers, not simply enlighten them.

Letters

These can be written from student to student about various aspects of the course and from student to professor or professor to student to clarify learning.

Interviews

Students can interview one another on key course concepts; they can also interview older or more experienced students, the instructor or other faculty members, experts on campus, and representatives of business and industry. Typically, interviewing involves considerable workaday writing, including writing down questions beforehand, taking notes, summarizing or abstracting from notes, and compiling material into a report, oral or written.

25

FIGURE 1

SOME FORMS FOR "WORKADAY" WRITING

Class notes
Reading notes
Field notes
Observations
Journals
Learning logs
Observation schedules
Free writings:
   Prior to lecture/discussion
   In process
   Postwrites
Questions/answers
Microthemes
Reading reports
Abstracts, summaries, précis
Notes and letters
Written debates
Soapbox
Class newsletter
Requests for
   information
   services
   clarification
Applications
Lab reports
Progress reports
Recitation notes
Annotated bibliography
Rebuttals
Evaluation
   of learning
   of unit or course
   of personal performance, growth, and learning

Add forms specific to your discipline:

_____

_____

_____

_____

_____

Class Newsletters

These can be done simply and quickly on a mimeograph or spirit duplicator, and they serve as a record of common learnings. In small classes, each student can, from time to time, prepare a one-page article, summary, review, or collection of ideas and quotes and bring in enough copies to distribute to the class. In larger classes, students can submit occasional contributions to a regular publication, or newsletters can be prepared among small interest groups. If computers are available, the newsletter can take the electronic form of a class bulletin board. More prosaically, a conventional bulletin board can serve as a place to post newsletter pages, questions, references, helpful hints about lab procedures, and so on.

Oral Composition

As I noted earlier, *composing* is a more basic skill than *writing*, and oral language activities can be extraordinarily useful in engaging students in learning. Further, oral activities often serve well as planning and preparation for writing. Useful oral activities can include reports to the class, small group discussions, "buzz groups" or brainstorming sessions, panel discussions, soapbox mini-orations, and short or formal debates. Often oral language activities will generate a need for more writing: a debate, for example, will require notetaking of various kinds, planning in writing, and written notes for rebuttals.

WORKADAY WRITING AND INQUIRY LEARNING

As I have described these workaday writing forms and their linkage with personal knowledge, the reader will no doubt have sensed my bias toward interactive and inquiry-centered rather than rote or formal learning. I do not propose to tell content teachers how to go about instructing in their disciplines. I believe, however, that workaday writing works best when it promotes inquiry rather than mastery of fixed concepts. Further, I believe this focus on inquiry is consistent with approaches being advocated in a great many disciplines.

Denny Wolfe of Old Dominion University has remarked that interest in inquiry is emerging, in part, because of changing paradigms of learning in the disciplines (104). He observes that the Aristotelian approach to knowlege was one of understanding the universe by breaking it into innumerable parts and providing labels for those parts—essentially a deductive process. For thousands of years, this atomistic approach worked well. More recently, however, scholars have become dissatisfied with the isolation of the disciplines (for example, C. P. Snow's *The Two Cultures*) and have argued for holistic, integrated views of knowledge (for example, Pirsig's *Zen and the Art of Motorcycle Maintenance*). We are coming to recognize that knowledge is more than the sum of an infinite number of parts or labels. We have also come to realize that what one sees is partly a reflection of how one wants to see (for example, Thomas Kuhn's *The Structure of Scientific Revolutions* [62]).

While such issues are by no means settled in the disciplines, the movement away from atomism toward holism, from rote learning to integrative and synthetic learning, comfortably meshes with current views of rhetoric, writing, and knowing. Language is bound up with learning, and the learning of language is achieved through use, not through study of parts and labels. Through the simple vehicle of introducing more workaday writing in the course, the content teacher can help students develop the kind of vision they need to know their discipline in the truest, most liberal sense. In the process, they can become better writers, too.

3. Writing Projects in the Disciplines

Workaday writing (as I have somewhat unglamorously described it) is a way to elicit more writing in the content areas without over-burdening the instructor with papers to correct. Writing in the content areas should go beyond the use of notes, journals, and free writes, however. Once instructors have tried a few workaday as-signments, they can consider developing more involved writing pro-jects. At this point, the pedagogy becomes a bit more complicated, but the use of writing in the content areas becomes proportionally richer and more exciting.

In her review of school and college content-area writing projects, Yates (105) found instructors doing some of the following projects to enhance learning in their fields.

In *science*, students have written evaluations of junk food nutri-tion, handbooks on health and diet, science fiction and science fact papers on ''star wars'' missile systems, descriptions of mathemati-cal and scientific principles applied in everyday life.

In *foreign languages*, students have prepared collections of word games in the language, written foreign language songs, created re-views of foreign language books and magazines (written either in English or the target language), and prepared reports on art, dance, traditions, and folklore in the foreign culture.

In *history*, students have written a range of local histories, in-volved themselves in letter-writing campaigns on current issues, created fictionalized news broadcasts about historical events, and written reports on the history and impact of science and technology.

Nor are content-writing projects limited to subject-matter classes. Yates found a number of English teachers incorporating ''real-world'' and subject-centered assignments in their classes, including position papers on issues in science and politics, analyses of com-munity problems, studies of popular culture, imaginative science fiction, and studies of career opportunities.

In contrast to workaday writing, these longer writing projects are reader- rather than writer-based. They demonstrate mastery of the subject for an audience that may be the instructor, peers in the class, or readers outside the school or college classroom. Thus they require more planning and organizing than workaday papers, which, in turn, creates a need for more and different learning in the discipline.

ASSIGNMENT MAKING

Many writing projects go astray at the beginning through failures of assignment making. Commonly (and understandably), the inexperienced writing instructor gives students a set topic, states an expected length and a due date, and waits for students to turn in papers. For example,

- Write a one thousand-word paper explaining the three forms of the lever.
- Discuss the effects of the OPEC oil embargo on the American economy.
- Write a paper on the effects of acid rain.

Such assignments, especially if given without backup from the instructor, may invite bad writing. What is to be the purpose of the writing? Who are the real or imagined readers? What is the student supposed to demonstrate? With assignments that lack a more precise focus, students often create incoherent prose, not because they do not know the material or how to write, but because they have no clear idea of what to do.

C. W. Griffin (43) has argued that a good assignment for content-area college courses should include the following:

- consideration of an audience (real or imagined),
- the role that the writer must play,
- the meaning of the piece, and
- the conventions of the text (the final product) that will be produced.

Ann Gebhard (38) adds the criterion—perhaps obvious but in need of articulation—that a good assignment should allow for "integration and imagination" in pulling together subject matter knowledge.

The following is a description of a three-step procedure for assignment making that I have used frequently for content-based writing assignments in English classes and in numerous workshops in writing in the content areas. It draws on the precept from Chapter 2 to *keep content at the center of the writing process.*

1. *Set content objectives for learning.* The first step is not to think

about writing, but about *learning*. What do you want students to know or demonstrate? Good writing grows from clearly articulated objectives. Objectives might be broad and general—for an entire course and leading to a long term paper or report—or quite specific—focusing on learnings for a single unit and generating a short paper. This monograph does not deal with the form objectives should take. Sample objectives that seem to me clear (though general) and appropriate for content writing projects are these:

- Students will come to an understanding of the basic principles of the civil war (history, social studies).
- Students will understand the potential effects of nuclear power plants on the economy (physics, political science, economics).
- Students will know the basic ways in which land development influences the economy (land management, economics, business).

(Instructors in those disciplines may rightly quarrel with the value or phrasing of these sample objectives; the content teacher, not the monograph writer, is the expert best able to write sound goals. For readers following along with a pencil and paper nearby, this would be an appropriate point to pause in their reading and describe what they regard as some valid and important objectives in their own subjects.)

2. *List real-world writing forms in which such objectives can be demonstrated.* The stress on "real world" is important here. Part of the vagueness of much college writing comes from the fact that students often write generic "papers." By having students write real-world forms, one provides several of the criteria for a good assignment outlined by Griffin: a text or model of the final product, a sense of the audience for a paper, a role for the writer to play, a means of focusing content.

Figure 2 shows actual kinds of writing that can lead to good content projects. The list is open-ended, and readers can add discourse forms specific to their disciplines. What do "real" historians, physicists, economists write? What is the audience for their work? What role or *persona* does the writer take with that audience? I have learned from writing-across-the-curriculum workshops that *foresters* write such forms as *conservation reports*, *radio scripts* (for short public service broadcasts), and *environmental impact statements*; *psychologists* write *case studies* and *clinical reports*; *teachers* write *recommendations*, *evaluations*, and *instructional rationales*; *automotive technicians* write *systems analyses*, *inventory reports*, and *repair records*; and *physicists* write *lab reports*, *grant proposals*, *progress reports*, and *collegial notes*.

FIGURE 2

SOME FORMS FOR CONTENT WRITING

Edited journals and diaries
Biographical sketches
Letters:
   public/informational
   memoranda
   persuasive:
      to editor
      to elected officials
Proposals
Progress reports
Position papers
Editorials
Feature articles
Question-answer columns
Political columns
Critical reviews
Applications
Discursive footnotes
Annotations
Scholarly notes
Specifications
Briefs
Charts
Diagrams
Flowcharts
Tables
User's manuals
Maintenance manuals
Software
Software documentation
Financial reports
Minutes
Journal articles
Popular articles
Environmental impact
statements
Telegrams
Commentaries
Newspaper "fillers"
Fact sheets
Press releases
Case studies
Poster/slide/film displays
Critical reviews:
   books (including texts)
   films
   outside reading
   television programs
   documentaries

Utopian visions
Scripts:
   radio
   television
   dialogues
   documentaries
Story problems
Math puzzles and conundrums
Record books
Interviews:
   actual
   imaginary
Directions:
   how-to
   guides
   hobbies
   academics
Dictionaries and lexicons
Technical reports
Consumer reports
Informational monographs
Cartoons
Slide show scripts
Imaginative writing:
   poems
   plays
   stories:
      historical
      science fiction
      fantasy
      informational

Add forms specific to your
discipline:

_____

_____

_____

_____

_____

The point in listing such forms is *not* to create a number of rhetorical forms (or "hollow shells," to use Knolblauch and Brannon's phrase [60]) for mastery. Rather, it is to lend focus and reality to the writing task. However, the use of real-world writing forms has the advantage of encouraging students to become familiar with the writing done by professionals in their fields.

3. *Create one or more focused activities that require students to demonstrate your objectives.* 1 + 2 = 3. Taking the objectives (Step 1) and the writing forms (Step 2), exercise your imagination to create a specific assignment (Step 3). As the following sample assignments show, I like to create several options or possibilities, then give students a choice of ways of proceeding. The assignments created here superficially resemble those cited at the beginning of this section, but they are considerably more detailed and imply audience, writer's role, and focus on the subject matter.

Here is an elaboration of the assignment to analyze the causes of the Civil War, with several options:

> Your textbook lists the causes of the Civil War as X, Y, and Z. Based on your understanding of the war, write a review of that chapter for *Popular History* magazine, stating the ways in which you agree or disagree with the text. A critical review usually consists of 750 words, or about three typed pages.
>
> ### Or
>
> Write a letter of about the same length to the author of the text expressing your opinion.
>
> ### Or
>
> Imagine you are a northern soldier about to go off to fight in the Civil War. On the eve of departure, write a letter to your family or sweetheart explaining your reasons for going.
>
> ### Or
>
> Write the same letter as a southern soldier.

The nuclear power writing assignment might be specified in one or several of the following ways:

> All over the country nuclear power plants have been closed or delayed by legal actions. Write a position statement to be read to your class discussion group on either side of the following debate issue: "Resolved: the United States should prohibit building of nuclear plants for electric power production."

Or

Write a letter to the governor of your state setting forth your views of the effects (positive or negative) of nuclear power.

Or

Write a science fiction story set in the year 2010 in which you show your view of the future effects of nuclear energy on society.

Or

Write a proposal for what you regard as a sane approach to the development of nuclear power in this country. Consider the U.S. Congress as your audience.

In the case of the land development topic:

You are an advocate of housing development in your community. Prepare the text of a three-minute speech to the town council weighing commercial development versus natural land use.

Or

Write the same speech from the perspective of an economist concerned with fiscal growth in the community.

Or

Create an imaginary dialogue or argument between pro- and anti-development people at the town council meeting.

Many instructors fill out these kinds of assignments with a set of specifications for the writing: when it will be due, the length (if it is not implied by the assignment), the criteria for evaluation (more on that in Chapter 4), and any other constraints under which students will operate.

There is an element of make believe about many of these writing assignments. Although I have suggested that students should write for an audience, a readership of a Civil War family is obviously in the realm of fantasy. To some extent the hypothetical aspect of assignments is a by-product of the classroom. In the best of all possible worlds (most composition theorists agree), students would write, without the artificiality of assignments, exclusively for real audiences and self-selected purposes. We do not teach in that ideal world, and thus virtually all writing done in colleges and universities must be created under classroom constraints, including assignments and imaginary audiences. On the other hand, many content instructors quickly find issues or problems that invite students to write for *real* real-world audiences—a letter to the governor, a piece of research presented to the student governing board of the college, even notes and articles submitted to professional journals or popular magazines. Part of learning to teach writing in the content areas is discovering ways of meshing course objectives and writing activities so that this happens more frequently.

FROM ASSIGNMENT TO WRITING: THE WRITING PROCESS

Teaching writing does not end with making the assignment. Contemporary writing theory recognizes that students need guidance at all phases of the process of preparing a paper (6, 11, 24, 44, 54, 75, 106). Views of the stages or steps in the writing process differ, but here I present six:

1. Preparation for Writing
2. Organizing to Write
3. Writing
4. Revising
5. Proofreading
6. Presenting

I want to caution readers that, at first, these steps may seem excessively time-consuming. In fact, what is presented here is a fairly comprehensive catalog of current practices, with the expectation that content teachers will choose those that best fit their courses.

Preparation for Writing

An assignment is just the beginning of a writing project, a way of setting the ground rules and getting students to begin thinking. Too often the teaching of writing seems to hibernate at this point, with instructors passively waiting for papers to come in, at which point they can teach through error correction. In fact, there is a good deal of indirect teaching of writing to be done during the writing process, especially in the content areas, through teaching of subject matter. Students can even use workaday writing as they go about preparing longer writing projects, thus adding considerably to the amount of writing done in a course. (See Figure 3.)

A primary source of knowledge for college papers is the textbook. Active notetaking or journal writings can be useful in ensuring that students gain more than routine comprehension of the text. Many

FIGURE 3

PREPARING FOR WRITING

Classroom Activity or Writing Resource	Related Workaday Writing
Textbook reading	Active notes, study questions, discussion notes, queries
Lecture	Active notes, journals, questions and answers
Recitation or discussion	Free writings on selected topics, postwrites, notes of preparation
Questioning	Free writes: what do I need to learn about my topic?
Laboratory	Lab reports, journals, notes, postwrites
Interviews or questionnaires	Question writing, summarizing information
Data analysis	Analysis, interpretation, summary, critique, mapping
Reader impact statement	Free writing
Planning	Outlining or making notes, maps, Venn diagrams, lists, etc.

Note: Not all of these workaday writings are required for all writing projects. Many projects will naturally lend themselves to other "in-preparation" activities than those listed here. It is frequently useful to have students save all the in-process writings for future reference.

texts, however, are written in a bland, factual style that gives the student no real sense of the vital issues in the discipline. They concentrate on covering accepted principles rather than discussing current issues or disciplinary processes. I encourage my students to carry their learning in preparation for writing beyond the text: "Find articles in popular magazines and scholarly journals. Look for a variety of print resources for your papers." A good nonfiction book or article on, say, a single aspect of the Civil War or urban planning can, I believe, convey a better sense of issues than the text. Coupled with personal notetaking, this reading can inspire imaginative writing.

In addition, through the use of outside materials brought to class, the instructor can do rhetorical analysis and modeling of writing in the discipline. Why do articles in a journal of landscape architecture take on a particular form? How are charts and graphs used in a home economics article? Why do some scholarly journals never use the first person or the active voice? In studying such pieces, the class should realize that the forms are not designed for slavish imitation. The customs, traditions, and stylistic oddities of writing in the disciplines generally serve functional needs. (The stuffiness of scholarly writing that avoids the first person is part of a nineteenth century tradition in which scholars wanted to make the results of their research look *absolute*. Such writing is gradually falling out of fashion, but students should understand why it is still accepted in some disciplines.)

It is sometimes appropriate for the content instructor to lead the class in a post facto analysis of how a scholarly or popular article came to be written. The instructor can also help students understand the processes and procedures of the discipline and how they lead to particular writing forms. What sort of research must have gone into a historical article on the holocaust? Where did the writer of an essay on space shuttle air purification get her information? How would a local historian have proceeded to learn about township schools 200 years ago? How did a study on ancient sailing vessels and their scientific principles work its way into print?

To deepen students' understanding of experience-into-writing in the disciplines, I often have content specialists come to my classes to talk about how they write, where they mastered their writing skills, and how they go from an idea to the printed page. Guests have included a local historian, a child psychologist, an urban planner, a computer specialist, a freelance writer, a museum curator, a newspaper feature writer, and a solar heating expert. Each one spoke with the class about how he or she gathers information, focuses it for an audience, and writes in accepted discourse forms. Without even bringing in outsiders, content specialists can do the same for their discipline and its knowing/writing patterns.

As students learn in preparation for writing, they should think about possible resources. My students prepare for learning with a series of questions to be answered in a free writing activity:

- What do you already know about your topic?
- What are the information sources for your past knowledge? How reliable are they?
- What *don't* you know? What do you need to learn?
- Where (in addition to the textbook) can you find answers?

Shirley Koeller (61) introduces the concept of *frame of reference* in science during this preparation for writing. She explains how scientists take an attitude or stance toward what they are viewing, and demonstrates how this point of view can affect what the scientist sees and discovers in the field. Then she has students seek to identify their own frame of reference in relation to the subject they are investigating. Doing this through workaday writing can help students gain perspective on the topic and on their role as writer.

As students prepare to write, they may even conduct experiments following either the natural science or social science models. Ideally, they should always have some hands-on learning in conjunction with their writing as a way to avoid the "encyclopaedia copying" syndrome—writing by shuffling quotations from other sources.

In summary, preparing to write can involve learning in diverse ways from diverse sources. If this preparation is done well, under the guidance of the content instructor, the next phase, *organizing*, goes smoothly.

Organizing to Write

As students move closer to writing a paper, they can begin to sift through their various notes and writings to find a point of focus, to organize their plan for writing. Barry Beyer of Carnegie Mellon University (6) involves his social studies students in what he calls "data analysis activities." First, he has students summarize data or information; then he has them explain the data "in terms of whatever else the student knows about the topic." He asks a series of questions—almost an Aristotelian set of categories—about the topic and students' knowledge of it:

- What is its place in a sequence?

What immediately preceded or followed?
What might have caused it?
What might it cause?

- How can this be classified or labeled?
    What is it similar to:
        in our personal experience?
        in fields related to our subject?
    If it is part of a pattern, what are its component parts?

- How has it changed?
    What is it becoming?
    What could it never become? Why?

- By way of contrast,
    How does it differ from others like it we have or know about?
    How does it differ from what we expected or feared?
    What, if anything, is self-contradictory about it?
    In what different ways can it be interpreted? (6, p. 188)

Naturally, such a rubric can be adapted for specific topics, drawing on the special features or concerns of the discipline involved. The point, again, is to get students analyzing and synthesizing information before writing.

Marilyn Hanf-Buckley (46) has students do this synthesis through "mapping." They create a graphic representation of how they see the parts of their learning as interconnected. (See Figure 4.) I have used similar maps or webs to have students plan or outline their writing. I try to eliminate the common misconception that there is only one right way to get a plan on paper—the formal outline with its Roman numerals and stair-step subheads. Ways of planning are many and varied. A few writers can plan in their heads and write nothing down. (I do not let such gifted people exercise their talent in my classes; I insist on seeing some written plan.) A few students can visualize their writing in the formal outline pattern they were taught in elementary school. (I caution them to avoid distorting their subject to make it fit the outline, a common problem among those who treat the outline as a rigid form.) My own style of planning (which I demonstrate for students) involves writing a set of more-or-less consecutively numbered points on a sheet of paper, with numerous arrows to represent relationships. I also show my students how I sometimes plan by shuffling a deck of index cards listing key points until I have an order that feels right. "Ballooning" (Figure 5) is another scheme I teach as a graphic

FIGURE 4

MAPPING

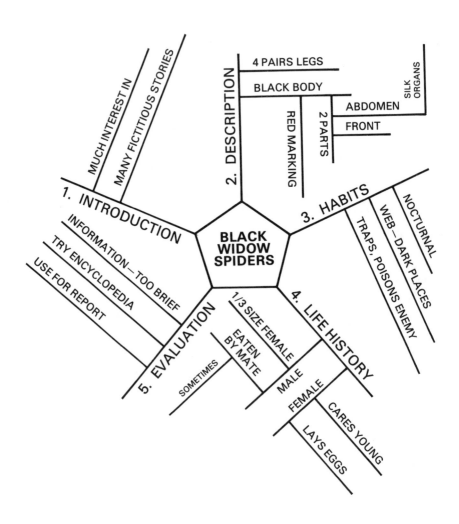

From "Mapping: A Technique for Translating Reading into Thinking," by Marilyn Hanf-Buckley, *Journal of Reading*, January 1971, p. 228. Reprinted with permission of Marilyn Hanf-Buckley and the International Reading Association.

FIGURE 5

"BALLOONING"
as a Planning Device

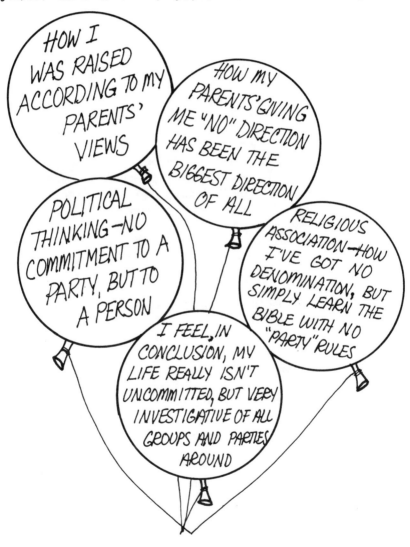

way for students to plan a paper. Each writer needs to find an individual technique for getting the plan down on paper.

At least as important as the form of the plan is getting students to think about what they want to accomplish in their writing. I generally have students do a short free write before they plan, a "reader" impact statement":

> Describe what you see as the central points you want to get across in this paper. What's important? What *impact* do you want this paper to have on the audience? How will people respond or react? What will they do or know or be able to do better as a result of reading?

In thinking about reader impact, students describe their aims and purposes for writing. As they discuss the central points to be made, they have practically completed their plan.

I preach the doctrine of "naturalistic order" when my students plan, again relying on my maxim "Keep content at the center of the writing process." Whether students are writing on extrasensory perception, electromagnetic levitation, or the process for manufacturing chocolate-covered cherries, ultimately the content of their subject will dictate the basic directions of their paper.

Freshman English instructors sometimes teach patterns of development—*comparison/contrast, examples, analogy, cause/effect,* and so on—and expect students to employ those patterns in writing. In reality, students do not need such formal structures, for they discover the patterns they need within their knowledge of the subject (as influenced by their aims in writing).

For example, the chocolate-covered cherries paper—which was written in my sophomore class—began by posing a question—"How do they get the liquid into the center of a chocolate-covered cherry?" In rhetorical terminology, this would seem to be a *question-answer* paper. Before the student answered his own question, however, he supplied the reader with results of a questionnaire he had administered. How did people in the street think chocolate-covered cherries were made? Now, I supposed, he was writing an *examples* paper. But then he included some information on his family's background in the chocolate industry, making the paper a *narrative.* Finally, he presented his answers in neat four-point fashion, *comparing* and *contrasting* the advantages and disadvantages of several manufacturing processes. The development of the paper, in short, followed a plan far more sophisticated than the kind usually outlined in a freshman composition handbook, but the student had discovered it intuitively, simply by knowing his subject well.

42

To repeat the central point, then: good plans for writing develop from knowing the subject well and from having a strong sense of the aim and purpose of the paper.

Writing

The moment of truth, for most writers, arrives when it is time to pick up the pen and write, when the learning and planning are complete (or nearly so) and a deadline is approaching. A great many students, like a great many of their mentors, dread this moment and delay it as long as possible. Some hide out in the research stacks, claiming they have not done enough reading (a common ailment among doctoral students). Others delay by finding other, presumably more pleasant, things to do. Although I nag my students to write their drafts long before the deadlines, invariably some writing comes in showing the signs of delay-it-till-the-last-moment.

Writing blocks are serious ailments, not easily cured. Many writers block because of bad past experiences: instructors who ridiculed them because of their writing or who marked every last error on the page. Blocking can also grow from laziness, for putting down words on paper in a precise order is exacting, hard work.

Writing in the content areas can be a cure for a good many writing blocks. Too often college students have been asked to make "bricks without straw" in writing classes, to write anything so that their writing can be evaluated and corrected. Good assignments in the content areas, those that have the sort of direction and focus I have described and are supported by solid planning, will give a majority of students the push they need to begin writing.

"When a writer sits down to write," said the British novelist Anthony Trollope, "he should do so not because he has to tell a story, but because he has a story to tell." Sounding like a modern-day Anthony Trollope, Chris Enke, a chemistry professor at Michigan State University, compares science writing to storytelling:

> An author writes a paper because he has a story to tell. The story has to have an introduction (the basis of the work), a narrative (the description and results of the work), and a conclusion (the interpretation of results). (30, p. 41)

Enke likens his own science writing to telling the story of his learning. In keeping with the conventions of science writing, he often removes the personal pronouns and narrative digressions from his writing, but he is essentially spinning a tale. "A scientific article," he continues, "is not only a vehicle of objective reality; it is a communication from a human/author scientist to a group of human/ reader scientists'' (30, p. 41).

To ease the fears of students, I often invoke Enke's storytelling metaphor, which can be extended well beyond the science laboratory. Students need to have an image of themselves as yarn spinners, not pedants, as they share their knowledge. At this point I also give my students examples of popular writing in the disciplines—articles from *Smithsonian*, for example—to show that one can write about complex subject matter in a form that is still personal and even conversational.

Other useful techniques that can be used to trigger the flow of writing:

- Have students look back through their notes and journals for personal responses and reactions to what they have read or studied. Often they will find the first paragraph or two of their writing already there, just waiting to be transcribed.

- Encourage students to talk through the opening of their paper, telling classmates or friends how they think they will begin. After explaining orally, they can overcome writing blocks by taking dictation from themselves.

- Let students free write their way into a paper, using stream-of-consciousness to put down anything that comes to mind. Among the free writing may be one or more sentences that will form the seed crystal for their paper.

- Have students write several opening paragraphs. They might begin with a quote, an outrageous statement, an assertion, or a plain and ordinary statement of thesis. Have them compare beginnings and choose the one that works best.

- Let students skip the very beginning and start writing with a paragraph from the middle. Often these middle paragraphs turn out to be the true beginning of the paper.

Word processors seem to help some writers in unblocking. Preliminary research suggests that students tend to write more on word processors than they do using pen or typewriter, perhaps because of the ease of revision, quite possibly because of the novelty of the video screen. Stephen Marcus (67) of the University of California uses word processors with the terminal screen dark as a way of helping students write their drafts freely and comfortably. With this ''invisible writing,'' he reports, students concentrate less on what they have written (and possible errors), more on what they are about to write. For student perfectionists who cannot move to the second sentence until the first one is exactly right, this seems an especially useful technique.

Many content teachers will not have time to teach unblocking strategies. To repeat an earlier point, the greatest help the instructor can give is to make certain that students know the material well before trying to write. Still, it is often useful to check up on blocked writers by having students do brief oral or written progress reports at this stage of the writing process.

Revising

The concept of revising is too little known among college students. In their schooldays, it often meant recopying a composition in ink. For such students, the idea that revising means changing content and form in a piece is foreign.

I introduce revision by using the contemporary example of a computer word processor. Word processors perform four basic operations: adding words to text, deleting words, substituting words, and rearranging blocks of text. Jonathan Swift, the British poet and satirist, seemed to know all about word processing (and revising) when he wrote:

> Blot out, correct, insert, refine.
> Enlarge, diminish, interline.
> *(On Poetry*, 1733)

I remind my students that they are "word processors" themselves, with or without a computer at their disposal. Revising is the stage where the writer examines a manuscript critically to see whether its parts hold together—to blot out, correct, insert, refine. I caution students that revision is not to be confused with proofreading, which comes later. Rubin correctly observes that skill in revising is related to skill in *reading*: "the capacity of students to perceive problems in their own writing and to make accurate decisions about revision" (85, p. 373).

Many students do not practice these reading/writing skills, in part, because revision is often something the teacher does for them. I aim to make my students independent editors of their own texts. Although I often collect papers at the draft stage and write responses (a topic discussed in the following chapter), my major concern is to teach Johnny and Jane to do editing and revising themselves.

A breakthrough idea in the teaching of writing during the past two decades has been the concept of *peer editing*, perhaps best articulated by Peter Elbow of the State University of New York at Stony

Brook (26). With training and instructor support, peers can often serve quite successfully as readers of each other's work. They can identify problems with organization, structure, accuracy of content, style, and correctness. Although peer editing consumes some class time, I find it time well spent and always build in a day for my students to share and critique drafts in the classroom. For the content teacher this time is not merely *writing* time, it is also *content learning* time, for the focus of such sessions should be kept on the knowledge and understanding of the paper and the clarity with which it is displayed.

Usually the peers are divided into groups of three to five students. Papers may be read aloud to the small group, or authors can be told to bring in copies for each group member. Peer groups need guidance and direction from the instructor; students should not simply be split into groups and told to "criticize" the papers. Figure 6 shows the kinds of questions students can use to focus their response to writing. Generally I chalk two or three major questions on the board as guidance for the sessions, then as the peers read and discuss, I circulate about the class monitoring results.

Revision is an easy stage for the content instructor to neglect, but it is an important one for both knowing and writing. Learning theory suggests quite clearly that people learn most when they do things right, not wrong. Focusing on revision allows students to write better drafts before turning in final copy. I also think that content instructors will find that revised papers in the disciplines will show greater knowledge of the subject matter; once again, then, good teaching of writing is bound up with good teaching.

Proofreading

Correctness is something that should be reserved for the last stage of writing. I tell students *not* to worry about spelling, grammar, and so on while they are drafting. Only after they have clearly shaped the content should they worry about surface correctness. In this way they do not distract themselves while revising or fritter away time dealing with relatively simple matters of correctness while more fundamental problems with content exist. Chapter 4 discusses the role the content instructor may play in identifying surface errors in student writing. In the spirit of making students independent editors of their writing, however, I stress that proofreading is the students' responsibility, not mine. Despite the doom-and-gloom reports of student illiteracies in the press, I have found that a majority of college students, even those in remedial tracks, have at

FIGURE 6

QUESTIONS FOR REVISING GROUPS

Note: Do not have students ask *all* these questions (or similar ones) at every revising session. Rather, pick some questions that seem most appropriate to your assignment and have the students work on two or three each time.

PURPOSE
- Where is this writing headed? Can readers clearly tell?
- Is it on one track, or does it shoot off in new directions?
- Is the writer trying to do too much? Too little?
- Does the author seem to *care* about his/her writing?

CONTENT
- When you're through, can you easily summarize this piece or retell it in your own words?
- Can a reader understand it easily?
- Are there parts that you found confusing?
- Are there parts that need more explanation or evidence?
- Are there places where the writer said too much, or overexplained the subject?
- Can the reader visualize the subject?
- Does it hold your interest all the way through?
- Did you learn something new from this paper?

ORGANIZATION
- Do the main points seem to be in the right order?
- Does the writer give you enough information so that you know what he/she is trying to accomplish?
- Does the writing begin smoothly? Does the writer take too long to get started?
- What about the ending? Does it end crisply and excitingly?

AUDIENCE
- Who are the readers for this writing? Does the writer seem to have them clearly in mind? Will they understand him/her?
- Does the writer assume too much from the audience? Too little?
- What changes does the writer need to make to better communicate with the audience?

LANGUAGE AND STYLE
- Is the paper interesting and readable? Does it get stuffy or dull?
- Can you hear the writer's voice and personality in it?
- Are all difficult words explained or defined?
- Does the writer use natural, lively language throughout?
- Are the grammar, spelling, and punctuation OK?

least moderately good proofreading skills. Nevertheless, they often fail to exercise those skills and thus submit error-ridden papers. In stressing student responsibility, I present my students with some practical guidelines to proofreading their own work:

- Buy a good *concise* handbook of grammar, usage, and style and learn to use it. (Most bookstores carry several different titles in this genre.)
- Get help with proofreading. (Recognizing that one has proof-reading problems and seeking help is not shameful. I do not regard students seeking help as cheating any more than I do my asking a colleague to scan a paper for my typos.)
- Use a spelling checker with your word processor, and a usage program if it is not too complicated. (These computer tools will not make a nonwriter into a writer, but they will help polish a paper, and I suspect they are part of the future.)
- Keep a notebook list of the words you commonly misspell and the usage items that trouble you.
- Proofread your paper three times, each time holding a ruler under each line to force yourself to look at every word. The first time concentrate on usage, the second time focus on spelling, the third time look for errors in capitalization and punctuation.
- Read your paper aloud before turning it in.

Presenting

The final stage of the writing process—at least as true writers experience it—is presenting the work to an audience or readership. Too often in college classes ''presentation'' simply means ''turning in the paper''—all papers folded vertically, please, with name in the upper left corner. The paper—the fruits of hours of labor—then disappears into the instructor's briefcase, to reappear days (or weeks) later with commentary and a grade.

Current composition theory suggests that as a way to experience the writing process fully, students ought to write for more readers than the professor. In content classes, this theory can also lead to enhanced learning as students test out their understanding of the subject by having audiences respond to their work.

In some cases, the audiences for content papers can be real readers, outside the classroom. As I write, my sophomore students are studying writing-as-persuasion. They are drafting letters, appeals, memoranda, and proposals that will be sent to legislators, newspaper editors, and leaders in business and industry. (Incidentally, I invariably discover that students' mastery of conventional English forms is greater when they write for such audiences.)

More often an audience will be the students in the course, a useful opportunity for them to serve as professionals in their discipline by responding to and criticizing final papers. The questions presented in Figure 6 can also be used here. In addition, students can do written critiques that focus on some of the following questions:

1. What is the main point? Can you summarize the central idea of this paper in several sentences?
2. Does the content of the paper seem accurate or truthful to you? Why or why not?
3. Is this paper likely to be successful with its intended audience? Why or why not?
4. What are the strong points? (Feel free to be lavish with praise.)
5. What are the weak points? (Be honest, but not hypercritical.)

If the "presentation" of papers is limited to the classroom, the instructor can ensure that this final step involves more than simply passing papers around the class for commentary:

- Have students in small editorial groups select one paper from their group for duplication and reading by the whole class.
- Collect "gleanings" from a set of papers—choice paragraphs, sparkling lines, well-wrought sentences—and duplicate them for the class.
- Create a bulletin board of particularly good papers selected by editorial groups.
- Put excellent papers in a looseleaf binder to keep on reserve in the instructor's office or in a departmental library.
- Create a class newsletter with editorial staff selected from the class to issue an occasional broadsheet with excerpts or whole pieces of student writing.
- If students are using compatible word processing systems, load selected themes into the memory of a public computer so that students can call them up and have a good read.

Once again let me repeat my concern that the content instructor not see this six-step process as impractically long. Whether or not the instructor spends any class time on the steps, students do *prepare, organize, write,* and (often) *revise* and *proofread.* Every paper is *presented,* even if the instructor is the only reader. This chapter argues the need to take the writing process out of the closet and provide students with some support at each phase. It argues further that the content instructor can ably assist with the process simply by focusing on course content as it emerges in writing. I urge content teachers to review this chapter from time to time and select different strategies to try in class, even while they are developing techniques of their own.

4. Evaluating Writing

Discussion of evaluating writing often makes content teachers edgy. First, they say, *evaluating* implies knowing a great deal about English, about rhetoric and grammar and good style, and content teachers may feel unfamiliar with these things. Second, they worry, *evaluating* conjures up the dreaded image of stacks of papers to be marked, an image that makes many content teachers avoid writing.

As for knowledge of criteria for "English" evaluation, the content teacher's knowledge of his/her discipline and its particular writing will provide the necessary skills to assess writing quality. The central question throughout evaluation is not, "Is this good writing?" (as measured on some absolute scale of literary excellence) but, "Does this writing effectively communicate learning in my discipline?" (a question that any competent instructor can answer with reasonable confidence).

The second reservation, with its image of a teacher toiling over piles of papers, is less easily answered. Assigning writing undeniably generates papers, and papers (except for some workaday forms) have to be read and commented upon by the instructor. However, when instructors in the disciplines do a good job of teaching learning in their subject (supplying students with straw to use in making bricks) and when they support the writing process from beginning to end as described in the previous chapter, the chore of theme evaluating is considerably reduced.

Before discussing specific classroom approaches to evaluation, I want to make a distinction between *evaluating* and *grading*. For many teachers, putting a grade on the paper is a primary concern, the end of the writing process. *Evaluating* is a considerably broader term; it may include the letter grade but is not limited to it. Further, evaluation can be done throughout the writing process, not simply at the end. (See Figure 7.) This chapter focuses on ways and means of evaluating writing.

EVALUATION IN PROCESS

The instructor can evaluate student writing at many points. Indeed, as Figure 7 suggests, evaluation can take place prior to actual writing, as the instructor assesses student questions and reactions to

FIGURE 7

POINTS OF EVALUATION
IN THE WRITING PROCESS

Stage	*Assessment Possibilities*
Assignment Making	Free writes in response to assignment, clarification (oral), questions by students, discussion of criteria of evaluation and grading
Planning	Student plans and written statements of aims, peer group review of plans, instructor approval
Writing (in-process assessment and evaluation of drafts)	Observation of writers at work (in class), peer group response, miniconferences, office hours, instructor-written response
	and
	Student, peer, and instructor assessment of surface correctness (proofreading)
Final Copy	Student self-evaluation, peer commentary and response, instructor response
Publishing or Presenting	Audience response

Grading

*1. Grade based on content only, with writing treated on credit/no credit basis.

2. Grading content and writing:

    *A. Analytic scales

    B. Primary trait assessment

    C. Holistic scoring

    D. Rubrics and checklists

    *E. Portfolio grading

    *F. Point systems

**3. Separate grades for writing and content by English and subject matter faculty

*Recommended   **Not recommended

the writing assignment: "Are they getting the idea? Do I need to supply more ideas and examples?" It can continue through the planning stages with students turning in a proposal or plan for approval. I especially recommend commenting on *rough drafts* of papers rather than focusing evaluation on a complete and *final product*. I find that students attend to comments on drafts much more carefully than they do when the instructor's remarks are "delivered" at the end of a writing project. Further, although commenting on drafts does consume time, it proportionally reduces the time spent evaluating at the close of a project.

In addition, commenting on drafts can be less formal and even less detailed than post facto assessments (especially assessments that must be linked to a grade). As a responder-to-drafts, I try to play the role of helpful reader or editor for my students. Instead of offering pronouncements about absolute value, I present observations: "I lose the train of thought here." "I enjoyed the introduction, but this next part struck me as less imaginative." "Is this fact correct? Where did you get it? Don't you need a footnote here?"

If the paper has previously been read and commented upon by the student's peers (a practice recommended in the previous chapter), I also make comments on the comments: "I think Joe has a good point here." "I see all your readers said you need more detail. I agree." "I understand what Sally is saying here, though the passage didn't bother me particularly."

Content teachers are in a unique position to offer helpful suggestions on drafts, in part because they are *not* burdened by rhetorical or "Englishy" knowledge. The subject teacher knows the discipline, the research, the material students are exploring through writing. He or she is thus in the best position to serve as a good editor by keeping content at the center of the evaluation process. Too, the content instructor knows the conventions of writing in the discipline and can help students discover them, offering advice that is well beyond the scope of the English professor—for example:

> "Although we don't use first person pronouns in journal papers in psychology, it's OK to use them in your lab report. Don't feel you have to call yourself 'the experimenter'."

It is important, too, for the instructor to realize that students are often frustrated by negative commentary. While one does not want to shield the writer from reality, little will be gained by harping on a student's failure or demolishing the student as writer and human being through sharp comments.

I focus my comments on the rought draft on the answers to two basic questions:

1. How can I respond positively to what has been done well and successfully in the paper (perhaps urging the student to extend points of excellence to the whole piece)?
2. What one or two pieces of constructive advice can I offer that will lead to direct improvement in the paper?

My aim is, quite simply, to do everything in my power as a teacher to help the student toward a successful writing experience.

For the content teacher, two additional questions are appropriate:

3. Is the material accurate; does it reflect sound learning in the discipline?
4. Is it presented clearly and effectively in writing?

Those two questions, if answered, will lead the content instructor to effective and natural feedback.

If time does not permit the instructor to take home papers at the draft stage, a good alternative strategy is to use peer editing—providing class time for discussion of drafts—coupled with a technique called "miniconferencing." While students work in their groups, the instructor moves about the classroom, monitoring discussions, answering questions as they come up in peer groups. If the instructor senses students having particular problems, he or she may actively intervene in a group (trying not to destroy the group's self-confidence) to shape its discussion or pull a student out of the group for a five-minute miniconference.

Another possibility for draft evaluation is to use office hours, either for required or voluntary conferences with students. Unfortunately, required conferences often become quite time-consuming. Equally unfortunately, voluntary conferences are usually attended by students who need them least. Nevertheless, if not planning to comment on drafts, the instructor should stress that the office door is open: "If you're having problems with your paper, be sure to come see me!"

Yates summarizes current practice on evaluation in process when she advises:

1. Give positive feedback whenever possible; point out strengths as well as weaknesses.
2. Use personal conferences for difficult or sensitive problems.

3. Respond to specific problems with specific suggestions for improvement. . .
4. Do not "grade" early drafts; reserve such judgment for final drafts.
5. Create sample "self-critique" sheets to help students guide themselves.
6. Give students some responsibility for evaluating each other's work. (105, p.15)

GRADING CONTENT WRITING

Before writing about putting numerical or letter grades on content writing, let me make the case for *not* grading the writing aspect of content writing. In contrast to many subjects, English composition does not have absolute standards for "good writing." As I have shown elsewhere, it simply does not work to teach students an inviolable set of rules and then to grade them up or down for their successes and failures in following those rules. Writing is too subjective for a clear and clean evaluation with grades.

Richard Veit of the University of North Carolina at Wilmington raises another good argument opposed to grading writing:

> Write whatever you will on a student's theme—the gentlest incentives to persevere, the friendliest offerings of alternatives for revision, the most painstaking explanations of rhetorical or mechanical content—once you place a grade on that theme, it will utterly dominate the discourse. (97, p. 432)

Because writing qualities are so subjective, grades (or at least any grade less than an "A") create arguments and counterarguments. My own convictions on not grading papers developed long ago in one of the first writing courses I taught, when one of my better students, who had been writing extremely well, received a "B-" for a subpar paper and that "negative" grade dominated the rest of our dialogue for the term.

Content instructors have one simple solution to the writing/grading dilemma: grade papers for *content* and place writing on a pass/fail basis.

Content instructors who use this plan make clear that high-quality writing is a course expectation, and they describe what they mean by quality writing: it is well planned and coherent; it has gone through drafts and revisions; it follows standard edited written English practices. Papers that do not meet those criteria (or any other set described by the instructor) are returned to the student for revision.Under this plan, writing is treated as a vital part of content learning, but the arbitrariness of grading writing is avoided.

Content instructors who prefer to grade individual papers might employ one of the six following grading schemes that have gained widespread acceptance in English and subject-area classes:

1. *Analytic Scales.* The traits of good writing (and knowing) are broken into categories as the instructor sees fit. A typical set of categories (evolved from Eblen's study [25] of what faculty value in student writing) might include *organization, development, grammatical form,* and *coherence.* Any number of categories may be created; they may cover content objectives as well as writing traits. Categories may also be weighted so that, say, content categories might lead to 60 percent of the grade while writing categories constitute 40 percent. Within each category the instructor makes a judgment on a scale that ranks the paper:

> Low   High
> 2   4   6   8   10

Scores for all categories are added to arrive at a grade. With a bit of juggling, the instructor can usually work out a scale that will lead to a total possible score of 100 or some other figure that students can readily translate into grades. (See Figure 8.)

2. *Primary Trait Scoring.* Under this scheme, the major objectives are described as "traits" of good writing—for example:

> Coherently expresses the principal cause of the Civil War.

In some schemes, a paper is simply rated yes or no as to whether it has the desired characteristic. Other evaluators prefer to introduce analytic scales for grading on the basis of whether a paper shows the desired trait to "no," "some," or a "considerable" extent.

3. *Holistic Scoring.* Holistic scoring acknowledges the subjectivity of writing assessment by resisting the temptation to fragment the writing into pseudoscientific categories. It is what most teachers have done with papers for years: they read the paper and form a judgment as to its "holistic" merit. Some instructors who favor this kind of scheme nevertheless articulate to students in advance what the criteria of evaluation will be. This is no easy task, for it forces the instructor to state very explicitly the kind of paper he or she ex-

FIGURE 8

AN ANALYTIC SCALE FOR CONTENT WRITING

This sample scale attributes 70% of the grade to the successful explication of three content objectives, one weighted 30%, two others valued at 20%. An additional 30% of the grade is attributable to writing quality, divided equally among organization, clarity, and correctness. Space is left after each category for instructor comments.

Content Objective A (30%)

$\qquad$ 2　4　6　8　　10 × 3 = $\underline{\hspace{3cm}}$

Comments

Content Objective B (20%)

$\qquad$ 2　4　6　8　　10 × 2 = $\underline{\hspace{3cm}}$

Comments

Content Objective C (20%)

$\qquad$ 2　4　6　8　　10 × 2 = $\underline{\hspace{3cm}}$

Comments

Writing (30%)

Organization (10%)　2　4　6　8　10　　　$\underline{\hspace{2cm}}$

Clarity (10%)　　　 2　4　6　8　10　　　$\underline{\hspace{2cm}}$

Correctness (10%)　2　4　6　8　10　　　$\underline{\hspace{2cm}}$

Comments

TOTAL　$\underline{\hspace{2cm}}$ of 100

Overall reaction and suggestions:

pects. Holistic scoring should always be supported by extensive commentary; it is not fair to students to place a grade on the paper without explaining the holistic judgments that led to it.

4. *Rubrics, Scales, and Checklists.* Pearce (78) has suggested that content teachers can develop their own schemes for evaluation and grading. A "rubric" is a list of what the instructor sees as the characteristics of low- and high-quality papers. Ideally, a rubric should be presented to the class prior to grading, but it may also be offered as an attempt to explain holistic scoring. Scales and checklists are simply various ways of breaking the qualities of good writing and good content into components so that the instructor can evaluate them one at a time. A checklist may even include evaluation during the process of composition, so that students might be assessed on the strength of their plans and drafts as well as their final product.

5. *Writing Portfolios.* Popular with English instructors, portfolios (or collections of writing) can be graded in a number of ways. Using holistic scoring or analytic scales, the instructor might rate a portfolio on such contents and traits as number and general quality of workaday writings, satisfactory completion of a journal, kind and number of critical reviews and outside readings, drafts of major papers, demonstrated growth from the beginning of the term to the end.

6. *Point Systems.* In this scheme, successfully completed papers receive points toward an overall grade. Workaday papers, journals, and notes may be credited, along with writing projects and essay examinations. The student is thus encouraged to write frequently and to write well. The instructor determines how many points (and how much writing) must be done to earn an "A," a "B," or a "C."

Each of these six grading approaches has a single trait in common: specificity of criteria. Their popularity seems to come about because they make the aims of writing instruction clear to students and articulate some of the mysteries of composition. Although these grading plans are popular, however, I want to repeat my appeal for content instructors to avoid grading the writing aspect of content writing at all. Despite the appearance of objectivity that these schemes present, they are still vulnerable to the major criticisms of grading student writing.

Also to be avoided, I believe, is the practice of creating a division of labor between English and content faculty members, with the English instructor reading and marking for writing quality, while the content teacher supplies a grade for knowledge of the discipline. Such a practice is counterproductive, I believe, because it isolates writing from content and implies that subject matter knowledge and the language in which it is expressed are not interrelated.

THE ISSUE OF CORRECTNESS

This section is potentially the most inflammatory in this monograph, not because it presents a particularly radical position, but because errors in surface correctness—spelling, punctuation, mechanics, usage—make many college instructors see red. The reasons are myriad, but they often rest with the notion that "correctness" in language is the mark of an "educated" person and that failure to write "properly" marks a persons as illiterate or slovenly.

Concern over errors has been around for a long time; in our language, it can be traced to the rise of London English as a prestige dialect in the thirteenth and fourteenth centuries. And for about as long a time, students have come to college writing less than letter-perfect prose. College instructors have complained about these errors, and they have blamed the lower schools for their failures.

I suggest that the complaining has done little good in the past, and that the prudent and responsible course of action is for the colleges to teach their students at the skill levels demonstrated by students on their arrival. I also believe, however, that content-area writing projects can serve a very real and useful purpose in giving students a sense of the importance of correctness.

I do *not* recommend that content-area instructors purchase red pens and become markers of every error in a student's paper. Rather, I suggest that instructors in the disciplines focus their concerns for correctness primarily on those aspects that affect comprehension in the discipline. That is, faced with a student who spells abominably, writes in nonstandard forms, and does not know a semicolon from a quotation mark, the instructor should focus on those errors that directly interfere with expression of content. Thus if the student misspells words for key concepts in the discipline, the instructor corrects them. If a dangling participle makes it unclear whether the experimenter or a chemical compound is to be heated to the boiling point, the teacher explains the confusion. If the student fails to use quotation marks when citing a major figure in the discipline, the professor inserts them (and includes a brief lesson on proper footnotes, if necessary). But the content instructor should not feel compelled to become the classic Ms. or Mr. Fidditch who corrects every error on the page.

I know from past experience that many content teachers will feel uncomfortable with this idea. "If I'm going to assign writing," they have told me at workshops, "then I feel a need to correct the errors I see." While I can understand such an attitude, I feel that a policy of correctness-in-content is superior for three reasons:

1. Composition research shows rather conclusively that blanket error correction seldom improves student writing. Selective correction works better (105).

2. Many content instructors will not teach writing at all if they feel they have to be grammarians.

3. Correcting errors that directly affect meaning in the discipline gives students a better sense of why errors are important than does blanket correction.

Perhaps most important is to stress that, in the end, students themselves must be responsible for correctness in writing. Content teachers may guide them and make correctness a part of the criteria for acceptable papers, but they should never become mere proof-readers. They have more important skills to teach in the content areas.

Lastly, I believe it is very important that instructors give careful consideration to the linguistic backgrounds of students, particularly those whose native language is not English or who come from communities where standard English is not commonly used. Speakers of dialect and other languages will, of course, need to make accommodations to function successfully in a world where money and power and prestige are controlled by speakers of standard English. But in "educating" people, we must not eradicate the language and culture they bring with them.

A NOTE ON EVALUATION THROUGH WRITING

Many advocates of writing in the content areas have made a case in favor of essay examinations over short-answer and multiple-choice tests. Essay examinations, they argue, show students that writing matters and evoke better demonstrations of subject-matter mastery than other test forms.

In principle, I agree, and in practice, I encourage content teachers to develop essay examinations.

If not designed carefully, however, such examinations can undercut a good writing program. In contrast to this monograph, which is devoted to ways of helping students write throughtfully about their discipline, examinations often force writers to create hurried, panic-stricken prose. I have been amazed to see the low quality of writing that essay examinations can evoke from students I know to have fully developed writing skills.

The following suggestions will help content instructors design examinations that reinforce good writing practices:

- Look for examination questions that require students to synthesize information rather than simply recite from the text or lecture.
- Study the traits of "good assignments" in Chapter 3 and apply them, insofar as possible, to the essay examination. For example, a good essay question may
  — invite students to write in a real-world discourse mode, such as creating a dialogue or imaginary letter.
  — encourage students to write to an audience other than the instructor, such as politicians, leaders in business and industry.
  — have students take on a clear-cut role and stance toward the subject matter, such as role-playing a specialist in the discipline.
- Don't overload students. One good question that involves careful synthesis of learning can reasonably be answered in an hour. To choose three out of five short questions and write successfully on them under examination pressure is unrealistic.
- State the criteria of evaluation plainly before students write. Include the criterion that the quality of the writing is integral to answering questions successfully.
- Talk through the examination during the preceding class session. Make certain students know that it will involve essay writing and that you will be evaluating writing quality.
- Use take-home and open-book/open-notes tests as much as possible. In the real world, we write with our academic material—our books and notes—beside us. Few people write on content-area topics strictly from memory.
- Consider announcing topics beforehand, in general, if not specific, terms. If an examination question calls for genuine syn-

thesis of learning, there is no harm in giving students time in advance to frame their ideas.

At their best, essay examinations can nicely augment a content writing program, but they must be designed and administered with caution. They also need to be evaluated with care. If the thrust of a course has been toward synthesis of knowledge through writing, but the final (essay) examination is graded for rote knowledge, much of the value of earlier writing activities will be lost.

5. Examples of Content Writing Projects

This chapter offers concrete examples of content-area writing projects. Each example includes not only a description of the writing project, but an analysis of how and why it meshes with current thinking and research on writing in the content areas.

THE QUEST PROGRAM

The QUEST is an approach to learning and writing that I have developed for a course in Interdisciplinary Inquiry at Michigan State University. The course is taken by senior students in mathematics, natural science, social science, and English who are enrolled in an Academic Learning Program offered by the College of Education. Academic Learning takes as its philosophy the merging of content knowledge and pedagogical learning for prospective teachers. Students enroll in my Interdisciplinary Inquiry course toward the end of the program; it is intended to help graduating seniors synthesize their view of the discipline they are about to teach and their ways of teaching it. In addition, it aims to help these students remove some of the disciplinary blinders they have developed in the course of four years of increasingly specialized education. Many have become locked into habits of viewing issues only in terms of their discipline; my objective is to have them learn (or relearn) interdisciplinary ways of seeing.

The QUEST is a project that students complete during the early weeks of the course; then they go into area junior and senior high schools and lead secondary school students on QUESTs of their own. The project proceeds in three stages, with content-area writing woven into each:

1. Questioning
2. Finding resources
3. Reporting learnings.

These are shown on the schematic (see Figure 9).

Virtually any broad topic in any discipline can serve as the focus for a QUEST. Most important is that members of a group find

FIGURE 9

QUESTING
An Approach to Interdisciplinary Inquiry

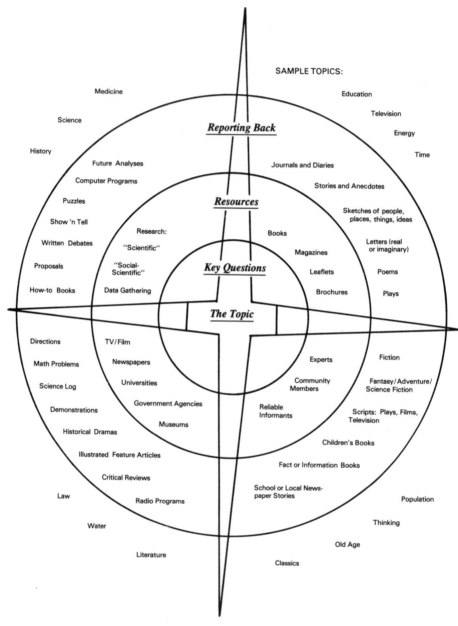

SAMPLE TOPICS:

Medicine

Education

Science

Television

Energy

History

Time

Reporting Back

Future Analyses

Journals and Diaries

Computer Programs

Stories and Anecdotes

Puzzles

Resources

Show 'n Tell

Sketches of people, places, things, ideas

Research:

Books

Written Debates

"Scientific"

Magazines

Letters (real or imaginary)

Proposals

"Social-Scientific"

Key Questions

Leaflets

Poems

How-to Books

Data Gathering

Brochures

Plays

The Topic

Directions

TV/Film

Math Problems

Newspapers

Experts

Fiction

Science Log

Universities

Community Members

Fantasy/Adventure/ Science Fiction

Demonstrations

Government Agencies

Reliable Informants

Scripts: Plays, Films, Television

Historical Dramas

Museums

Children's Books

Illustrated Feature Articles

Fact or Information Books

Critical Reviews

School or Local Newspaper Stories

Law

Radio Programs

Population

Water

Thinking

Literature

Old Age

Classics

some points of contact with it to enable them to relate it to their own interests. In doing this project with senior undergraduates (and with some secondary school students) we have ambitiously taken on the entire known universe by proposing a QUEST on the classical Greek partition of the elements into *air, earth, water,* and *fire.* College students have selected other QUEST topics, including *classics,* the *population explosion, right-to-life, schooling,* and the *nuclear future.*

In the first stage, students generate a series of questions for investigation. We write the selected topic in the center of the chalkboard and brainstorm to generate strings of related questions. Eventually I divide the class into small interest groups, each one selecting an aspect of the topic (say, *earth, fire, air,* or *water*) and doing another more detailed question web of its own. I stress that the writing of good questions is a central part of learning. After several class periods, the questions are refined and each student arrives at a question to investigate in some depth.

Finding resources is the next stage. As an English professor I am, of course, interested in library resources, and I review ways of using the university library successfully. Curiously, many students—even seniors—do not use the library very effectively or creatively, perhaps because they have seldom been asked to research questions of their own invention.

I also place strong emphasis on nonprint resources. A journalist once told me that newspaper people seldom stop first at the library. "Get on the phone," he advised. "Find out who knows something about the topic and ask." Therefore I encourage students to think about human resources: experts on campus, community members, people who can be reached by telephone. *Interviews,* of course, require considerable workaday writing, but they are a powerful learning tool, and college students enjoy doing them.

In addition, *institutions* can often be good resources: museums, government agencies, newspapers, businesses and industries, media. Students can brainstorm for possible institutional resources to aid them in their QUEST. We also discuss *research* as a learning resource—defined simply as "what you do when you can't find answers anywhere else." Although time and facilities in the course are limited, most of my students conduct some research to support their study—usually of a social science nature using interview schedules or questionnaires. Once again, such investigation involves writing. This view of research, incidentally, helps cure students of a school- and college-induced notion that "research" means going to the laboratory and filling in blanks in a laboratory workbook. They come to see that research involves questioning and seeking, not just proving the already known.

The final stage, reporting back, involves writing in the content areas (although I do not use that term with my students). I suggest that there are many ways in which information can be reported to a group. In the three years I have been conducting the program, my students have created fiction, drama, simulated radio broadcasts, proposals, position papers, children's books, computer programs, posters, and a variety of demonstrations. Each of these projects goes through the stages of the writing process, including data analysis, planning, drafting, peer editing, and so on.

The QUEST is, for me, a model of learning in most disciplines with its phases of questioning, finding answers, and reporting to others. It is also fundamentally linked to language use, in general, and to writing in the content areas, in particular. The phrase "writing in the content areas" is never used in the Interdisciplinary Inquiry course however; it is simply a natural part of the process.

TEACHING SCIENCE WRITING

A colleague at Michigan State, Fred Carlisle, has developed a three-term freshman writing course for science majors. First introduced in the mid-1970s, it remains a popular alternative to the mainstream freshman English course (14). The focus in English 104, Writing for Science Majors, is primarily on finding one's voice and identity as a writer, rather than on writing for and in the sciences. Students keep journals and diaries of personal experience; their initial writing assignments focus on autobiography, reminiscence, memoir, and narrative. (This emphasis is shared by all of Michigan State's freshman courses; the intent is to make students secure as writers from their own experiences before moving to academic writing.) Toward the end of the term the assignments shift toward expository and analytic writing, and students "have written in detail about telescopes, derivatives, different kinds of bicycle wheels, curve balls, isomers, and chess, as well as about their interest and knowledge in science" (14, p. 38).

In the second term, English 105, The Scientist as Writer, students explore a wide range of discourse written by scientists, including popular writing and fiction. They look at writing by James Watson and Francis Crick, Thomas Kuhn, Loren Eiseley, P. B. Medawar, David Bohm, and others on topics that include the social and political implications of science. Through this reading they come to see scientists (and science writers) as human, as makers of language. The writing includes an interview with a scientist, a critical review of some of the reading for the course, an argumentative paper on a science topic, and may extend to imaginative writing such as science fiction.

The third term, English 106, Introduction to Scientific Writing, zeroes in on "functional prose—clear, direct, unambiguous, and fitting" (14, p. 39). Given the careful preparation of the first two terms, however, students are now in a position to see writing in the sciences as a process, not just a matter of filling in prescribed forms. They write scientific papers, popular articles, instructions, research proposals, lectures, and other modes of science writing. The course, then, smoothly integrates content and "English," leading the way, as Carlisle explains, "across the unexplored territory between science and English" (14, p. 39).

THINKING BEFORE WRITING
IN PUBLIC RELATIONS

Writing in *Journalism Educator*, Marilyn Fregley and John Detweiler (35) of the University of Florida have described the writing program they have developed for majors in Public Relations. Too often, they say, PR students think that getting publicity for a product or project is simply a matter of typing up a press release and sending it on its way. To teach the realities of this kind of writing, they have students create public relations "firms" in class, secure clients, and create a "model sampler" of PR material. Along the way, students engage in thorough and careful analysis of audience, content, and medium.

For example, students make a study of the "gatekeepers" in media: the TV, radio, and newspaper staff members who routinely sift through public relations material selecting the items that reach the public. The writers then prepare a variety of press releases, taking different slants and angles to reach diverse media. Students analyze the tone of previously published press releases to discuss appropriateness, and they critique stories written by class members to select those that are most successfully written.

Looking at different public relations discourse forms, students examine "wooden" brochures and practice rewriting copy. They also design a "storyboard" for a commercial and write spot announcements for public service work.

Finally, they write a position paper on a topic for public relations and present it to their classmates in a role-playing situation, with peers taking the roles of media people at a press conference. The writers are grilled by their peers and thus learn a final lesson about writing for audiences. These simulations are also videotaped for analysis and discussion after the fact.

The Fregley/Detweiler program impresses me because of its thoroughness, the use of simulation of real-world writing, the diversity of writing done by students, and especially, the stress on careful analysis of audience.

SOCIAL ACTION PORTFOLIO

I have adapted the Fregley/Detweiler approach to my own intermediate writing course for sophomores, juniors, and seniors who come from many disciplines and majors. It is useful, I think, for every citizen to know something about how to use writing to promote an idea, issue, or cause. My assignment is for students to—

> Choose an issue or topic that you feel has significance for a large number of people in society today. Prepare a portfolio of at least five writings that clarify your position on the issue and seek to persuade other people to share your point of view.

Among the issues students have selected are abortion/right-to-life, treatment of the aged, pornography, values of the young, child abuse, and sports ethics. I announce the project well in advance and urge students to start a clipping file of related newspaper and magazine materials on their topic.

I require the position paper as the first item in each student's portfolio. Where I generally encourage students to use informal essay organization, avoiding the rigid point-by-point analysis, I have them do the position paper in a highly structured, "Dale Carnegie" manner: tell them what you're going to tell them; tell them; tell them what you've told them. The position paper serves to focus the writer's attention and values, and provides a jumping off point for other writings that may include the following:

Letters:
    to editors
    to political leaders
    to influential people
Editorials
Columns
Proposals (for laws or actions)
Critical reviews (of books, articles)
Broadsides (one-page fliers)

Posters
Advertisements and commercials
Press releases (for TV, radio, newspaper)
Feature articles
Public service announcements
Brochures
Memoranda (to other citizens)
Fact sheets

The portfolio is developed over a two-week period in which the class functions as a workshop: students bring materials to class and write and revise on the spot. I review a preliminary proposal for the portfolio and read each piece of writing, in class, at least once.

I also urge students to make as much of the writing as possible aimed for a *real* audience. Thus many of the letters written for the portfolio are mailed, columns are submitted to the university newspaper, broadsides are duplicated and posted about the campus.

LANDSCAPE HISTORY

John Stilgoe of the Departments of Visual and Environmental Studies and Landscape Architecture at Harvard engages his students in inquiry-centered learning that has them study and write about interesting aspects of the history of architecture (9). Landscape history, he suggests, contains history in miniature, since "every historical period lives however faintly in the contemporary American landscape" (9, p. 12). He has his students search secondary materials for ideas about various facets of landscape history; they look at "old periodicals, travel narratives, local histories, . . . government publications . . . old photographs, postcards, silent films, and advertisements." Then they look outside the classroom for examples of existing architecture that illustrate their topic. Among Stilgoe's fascinating suggested topics are these:

"The development of the 'rumpus room'
The re-use of railroad stations, schools, gas stations . . .
The rise and fall of ceilings . . .
The development of sports facilities in public parks
The cult of the swimming pool . . .
Children's street games . . .
Farm artifacts in modern suburbia." (9, p.13)

He reports that very lively writing results from this project, and several of his students have had their papers published.

SIMULATIONS AND CASE STUDIES

Making writing "real" for the student who must complete it to satisfy college course requirements is often difficult. No matter how much the instructor stresses real-world connections, for some students school writing is school writing, and it comes out lifeless and dull. One useful strategy for increasing the reality of writing is to use simulations and case studies, either separately or in tandem.

In teaching high school English, for example, I engaged students in a simulation called "The Dennison Dilemma" (56). Students receive a case study of the fictional town of Dennison. The town must decide whether to grant a zoning waiver for a company that proposes to manufacture automobile bumpers in a factory to be located along the banks of the beautiful Dennison River. This simulation leads to a role-play of a town meeting, but it involves considerable reading and writing as preparation.

Lynn Troyka and Jerrold Nudelman (94) of Queensborough Community College have written a very useful college text, *Taking Action*, that develops a variety of simulation games, all designed to enhance communications skills. Their games include "Uprising Behind Bars" (prison unrest), "Conservation Crisis" (pollution), "Dollars on Demand" (economics and government), "Taxis for Sale" (economics and business), "Women on Patrol" (social science), and "Population Control" (science and social science). This book also provides the content teacher with a model for developing simulations and simulation games, as well as ways of integrating reading, writing, listening, and speaking activities.

William McCleary (69) of Genesee Community College is one of many writers to describe the use of the case study as a starting point for student writing. He reports having used case studies to teach writing in such diverse areas as law, history, and hospital management. In contrast to the simulation, which casts students in dramatic roles and involves class interaction, the case study presents a real or hypothetical situation to which students write appropriate responses. Illustrating his approach for a course in sociology, McCleary shows how the instructor can present case studies of social deviance that lead to carefully researched analytic writing. A case study can, in fact, be written for almost any problem in any discipline.

SCIENCE DIALOGUES

John Wilkes (103) at the University of Southern California at Santa Cruz found that students were often failing to internalize science concepts from their classes. He tried having them write dialogues—actually radio scripts—between "a scientist and an intelligent, eager-to-learn, but ignorant friend" (103, p. 58). After analyzing radio interviews of this "genre"—the radio science featurette—he set down the following rules for his students:

1. Make the dialogue three and a half minutes long (about 600 words). . . .
2. Give each character about ten speeches, which should correspond roughly to ten questions raised by the scientist's friend.
3. Give both characters about the same number of words to say. In other words, don't let the scientist dominate the conversation. . . . (103, p. 58)

Wilkes emphasizes that his aim was to engage students in creating popular science writing, not "scientific" writing intended primarily for members of the scientific community. Following the rough guidelines, his students produced science dialogues on a wide range of topics. Two of the scripts—one on the potential for cities in outer space, the other on saving dolphins from tuna fishers—were broadcast by CBS radio, thus giving Wilkes's students a dramatic understanding that writing can and should reach audiences in the real world.

CONSUMER REPORTS

In the spirit of Wilkes's science dialogues, William Lewis (64) of Central Michigan University has engaged his students in real-world research that leads to technical writing for a popular audience.

In the Product Research Report students choose a product that is sold by a number of different manufacturers—for example, nail polish, lipstick, rubberbands, candy, ball point pen. Following Lewis's guidelines, students create a description of the characteristics of the product (a "definition" of the product to be examined), and then develop a set of objective tests for determining which of the range of products works best. After testing, students write a variation of the consumer report for their classmates. Aside from the firsthand research involved, this assignment is a good one because it uses the class as an audience of consumers.

Lewis's second assignment asks students to gather data to make a Survey Report of opinions on a current issue or problem. Students survey campus interests in such topics as motorcycle safety, grading systems, diets, drugs, the economy, and current films. First they analyze the topic, breaking it down into issues and subtopics. Then they generate a series of questions and refine them, through field testing, to create a viable opinion poll. After data collection, they develop papers reporting their results to the rest of the class, again drawing on the potential of the class as audience.

INTERDISCIPLINARY HUMANITIES

Writing across the curriculum lends itself naturally to interdisciplinary studies because of its emphasis on knowing, discovering, and making connections. James Beck (4) of the University of Wisconsin, Whitewater, has argued forcefully that writing can be used as a way of helping students remove the "disciplinary blinders" that increasingly force them to view issues and problems solely from the perspective of their major field or discipline. Students in his humanities class examine issues and topics as diverse as architecture, food scarcity, and the effects of technology. For each topic, they run through a kind of interdisciplinary checklist, forcing themselves to think about the problem from the perspectives of many subjects. What are the implications from, say, theology? or fine arts? or anthropology? or physics? or geography? In adapting Beck's approach for my own classes, I have developed an "alphabet of disciplines" (gleaned from the university catalog) from Accounting to Zoology for students to follow. The interdisciplinary perspective invariably leads to stronger, more informed writing than that produced through the vision of a single discipline.

A program developed by Judith Scheffler (86) and her colleagues at Temple University involves faculty from many subjects in interdisciplinary study with a deep concern for writing. During the summer, "freshmen ranging from remedial to honors level are invited to join four to six faculty members in an interdisciplinary group that will undertake a year-long study of a broad topic like 'The Environment,' 'The Human Condition,' or 'Law and Order.' " Remedial help is provided for those students who need it. The interdisciplinary content of the program provides rich material for writing, with the distinct advantage that content and English instructors are able to work together in guiding students to successful completion of assignments. All faculty participate in designing writing assignments. Papers are read first by an English specialist, and after revision, they are reviewed by one of the content experts in the program.

6. Programs in Writing Across the Curriculum

This chapter presents the writing of some colleagues who have done imaginative work in content writing and developing writing programs across the curriculum. No single program will fit all colleges and universities. As these writers show, each institution must survey its strengths and weaknesses and assess its needs and resources. Sometimes leadership for programs will emerge in the English department. At other times it will grow from the subject fields or from the administration. These offerings, then, constitute a sampler of what I regard as some of the best writing-across-the-curriculum programs in the country. Readers may find some aspects of these programs directly importable to their own campuses. However, these projects serve best as models of approaches to a problem rather than as generalized solutions.

MICHIGAN TECHNOLOGICAL UNIVERSITY
Art Young

During spring term in 1976, a biology teacher telephoned me to ask how a student could get a "B" in freshman composition and write such a poor term paper for a senior-level biology course. When we asked the student some questions about her educational experience, Mary revealed that she had never before written a term paper for biology and, in fact, had done very little writing beyond freshman composition. All the skills that should have been at her fingertips—researching the topic, establishing a purpose, organizing the material, revising earlier drafts, editing for usage—had been allowed to atrophy for lack of use. If writing effectively is an important part of being a scientist, then Mary should have been writing regularly—both to learn about science and to communicate about it—*in science classes*.

The biology teacher and I discovered another reason for Mary's poorly written senior report. She was poorly motivated and held incorrect perceptions about writing. She did not believe that she could learn about biology by writing about it. Nor did she believe that writing was important to her academic and career success. She was not going to be a writer or an English teacher, but work in a hospital or laboratory as a medical technologist. Writing was something she did in English and some liberal arts courses but not in science courses. Writing had nothing to do with being a medical technologist—she had been able to maintain a "B" average in her science courses, and she had written very little in those courses except to give some short answers on lab reports and quizzes. In Mary's educational experience, only English teachers seemed to care about writing.

Many of us on the faculty at Michigan Tech had to admit that Mary had a point. Catalyzed by our interview with her, then, we established a writing-across-the-curriculum program to remind ourselves as well as Mary and the rest of our students that we valued effective writing as an integral component of the inquiring mind, the educated person, the successful professional.

During the 1976-77 school year, the English faculty presented a proposal for a program in writing across the curriculum to our campus, received almost immediate endorsement from the administration and from colleagues in other departments, and conducted our first writing workshop for faculty in all disciplines.

The Philosophy

From the very beginning, our program was teacher-centered. We believed that we needed to establish a community of teachers who understood and valued the uses of writing in education. Only within such a community would students learn to value written language and develop their abilities to use it. Although we were influenced by numerous scholars in rhetoric and composition, we made the work of James Britton the theoretical basis of our program.[1] We especially liked Britton because of his assumptions on the discovery role of writing, his insistence on an expressive base for all writing, and his call for students to write frequently for a variety of purposes to a variety of audiences in a variety of courses. Britton's work seemed to provide a framework in which to approach the problems with student writing as articulated by Mary. We did not and do not insist that our English and non-English colleagues subscribe uncritically to Britton's theory, but we have found that a common theoretical base for instruction in writing has been invaluable for establishing cross-disciplinary communication about points of agreement and points of departure. Therefore we determined to work together with faculty in all disciplines in writing workshops. Whether or not participants found Britton's theory helpful, we hoped that certain principles would inform the workshop experience.[2]

1. *Writing is a learning activity as well as a communication activity.* Writing is an important tool *to learn* the content of the discipline as well as *to communicate* to others what has been learned. Teachers who, for one reason or another, are not able to assist students directly in improving their writing skills can still participate in a writing-across-the-curriculum program by having students learn the content of a course and make it their own by writing about it.

2. *In the learning situation, the writing process is as important as the written product.* When we think of writing, we often think of the finished essay or report, not the process that created it. But in the educational setting, where we are teaching students to write better essays and reports, we can do a more effective job by paying attention to the writing processes our students use. We can help students write better by making assignments that enable them to experience important aspects of the writing process: brainstorming, researching and selecting a topic, organizing and drafting ideas on paper, revising and focusing on a particular purpose and audience, and editing and proofreading to make the prose effective.

3. *Writing and reading are interrelated learning skills.* To develop flexibility and sensitivity in written language, students need to be active and versatile readers. Teachers in all discipines should work to improve student reading and writing abilities even as they teach the mastery of technical content, for in a very real sense these activities are inseparable. To be a good economist, social worker, or mathematician, is to be able to read and write like one.

4. *"Good writing" is nurtured and matures in a community that values written language.* Mary told the biology teacher and me that she did not feel a part of a community that valued her writing and that of others. She did not perceive the larger society as representing such a community, nor did she perceive her four years on our university campus as representing one either. Consequently, we have set out to create such a community at MTU. Our resolve has been strengthened by the growth in community spirit we are experiencing at Michigan Tech,[3] and by the expanding sense of community we have with teachers and students at other schools (elementary, secondary, college) who share the ideals of writing across the curriculum.

The Program

The writing-across-the-curriculum program at Michigan Tech has been in operation since 1977. We knew that we would not find a quick fix to improve student writing, and we have not. But we have found much that we did not expect to find—about student writing and learning, about teaching and research, about our colleagues and their disciplines, about ourselves and our discipline. In 1978 we received funding of $225,000 over five years from the General Motors Foundation. New internal funding has more than matched that amount. The external funding provided us with the time and resources to launch our program; the internal funding has enabled us to continue the program after the external funding expired. Some of the important components of our program follow.

1. *Workshops.* The faculty writing workshops have been the heart of our program. Thus far we have conducted 15 workshops for over 275 Michigan Tech faculty from all disciplines. Each multiday, off-campus workshop involves participants in writing, talking about writing, and rediscovering the role of writing in learning and in communication.[4]

2. *Curriculum.* A year of freshman English is required of all students. Because we believe that writing in specific disciplines is best done in those disciplines, we do not teach writing in the disciplines in freshman English. That is a liberal arts course in which students study and practice writing as a humanistic activity. However, such concepts as brainstorming, revision, and peer critiquing are introduced and practiced so that teachers in other disciplines can expect students to have certain writing experiences as they enter upper-level classes.

   We have greatly increased the number of sections offered of advanced writing courses. Almost all departments now require an upper-level course (technical writing, business writing) taught by English teachers.

   We also are implementing writing-intensive courses in all disciplines. These are courses that use writing to teach the traditional content of the course. Thus far the implementation has been more successful in some departments than in others. We still have a long way to go to make this concept an established part of the curriculum at MTU. We know, however, that many more teachers in all disciplines use writing to teach content after attending one of our workshops.

3. *Language Laboratory.* The university language laboratory serves

students enrolled in all courses, not, as in the past, just English courses. Students receive individual tutoring in reading and/or writing. All students are welcome, not only those perceived as "remedial." Almost all students can benefit from talking about their writing and then revising it as new discoveries and insights occur.

4. *Administration*. The program is administered by English faculty. We are responsible for conducting the workshops, arranging followup activities, publishing a newsletter, advising on curriculum, encouraging team-teaching projects, supporting collaborative research on writing and learning across disciplines, and evaluating the ongoing program. Faculty in other disciplines participate in the workshops and followup activities, make curriculum changes in their own departments, and join with English faculty on interdisciplinary teaching and/or research projects.

Research and Evaluation

Research and evaluation is an integral component of our program. A standing committee of seven interdisciplinary faculty (currently, two in literature, two in composition, two in psychology, and one in linguistics) has responsibility for program evaluation and program planning. We place evaluation and planning together because we want the results of our research and evaluation to influence the continued development of the program. This committee has just completed a two-year evaluation project that has been published as a book.[5] Committee members investigated the main aspect of our program, the writing workshops, by doing studies of faculty attitudes toward writing, their teaching practices, student attitudes toward writing, and their writing practices and abilities. They coordinated research by over 30 faculty from 10 different disciplines on large program components as well as on specific writing activities in individual classes. Some of the results were surprising, some were predictable, some disappointing, some heartening; we have learned about research in writing as well as about our program.

NOTES

[1] See James Britton's *Language and Learning* (Harmondsworth, England: Penguin Books, 1970); his *Prospect and Retrospect*, ed. Gordon M. Pradl (Montclair, N.J.: Boynton/Cook Publishers, 1982); and his book with colleagues Albert Burgess, Nancy Martin, Alex McLeod, and Harold Rosen, *The Development of Writing Abilities (11-18)* (London: Macmillan Education Press, 1975).

[2] For further information regarding the theory and practice of the Michigan Tech writing-across-the-curriculum program, see *Language Connections: Writing and Reading Across the Curriculum*, ed. Toby Fulwiler and Art Young (Urbana, Ill.: National Council of Teachers of English, 1982).

[3] For further information on the importance of community in developing a writing-across-the-curriculum program, see my "Rebuilding Community in the English Department," *ADE Bulletin*, no. 77 (Spring 1984): 13-21.

[4] For further information on the Michigan Tech model of faculty writing workshops, see Toby Fulwiler's "Showing, Not Telling, at a Writing Workshop," in *College English* 43, no. 1 (January 1981): 55-63.

[5] The book is entitled *Research Connections: Writing Across the Curriculum*, ed. Art Young and Toby Fulwiler (Montclair, N.J.: Boynton/Cook Publishers, 1985).

UNIVERSITY OF NORTH CAROLINA AT WILMINGTON

Margaret Parish and Colleagues

The English Department at UNCW began its commitment to writing across the curriculum several years ago through its sponsorship of a Faculty Writing Symposium at which speakers and workshop coordinators from Beaver College did effective evangelical work in raising the consciousness of faculty campuswide. In addition to the projects reported on the following pages, the UNCW Faculty Senate has appointed its own Committee on Writing Across the Curriculum, which in the course of a year and a half has published a monograph for the faculty entitled *Writing Across the UNCW Campus*, and proposed to the Senate a structured program of writing requirements for every UNCW student. The Senate has also moved that design and implementation of Writing Emphasis courses be explicitly included among the areas of professional performance relevant to academic preferment. (MP)

The Place of Writing in the UNCW Curricula

John F. Evans

Near the end of the fall semester in 1984, the UNCW faculty responded to a questionnaire distributed by the Committee on Writing Across the Curriculum. This report summarizes the information gathered in that faculty questionnaire.

Students can complete 95 percent of the credits toward the undergraduate degree at UNCW without writing more than their names or a letter of the alphabet. In fact, if current trends toward computerized testing continue, students will need only the ability to darken a rectangle on a computer card to demonstrate their proficiency in a field of study. Who can really blame students if they don't care that "they're writing ain't to good" when all the evidence tells them that nobody except Dr. Commasplice is concerned, and once rid of him they can forget it all?

"Forget it all" is exactly what students can do at UNCW if the recent WAC survey is an indication of the amount and kind of writing done on this campus. The most frequent kind of writing is still the essay exam, followed closely by short- and medium-length research papers. Despite the good efforts of a writing workshop (Spring 1983) and the publication of a writing brochure (1984), few of the fundamentals of recent writing theory are practiced by those who could have the greatest effect—classroom teachers.

79

Indeed, if the 99 responses to the questionnaire are any indication of interest in writing on this campus, it would be safe to say that less than one-third of the course offerings require any writing at all. Students are seldom required to write daily within their discipline, so they do not often get a chance to see writing serve its natural function in the learning process. Neither do they have much opportunity for peer review or rewriting; therefore vital steps of the writing process are ignored.

Writing English is the foreign language experience of undergraduate study on today's campus for several reasons; the most ironic is the one given by teachers who claim they do not assign writing any more because students cannot write. Then there are teachers who feel they are on the writing-across-the-curriculum bandwagon because they assign long term papers or give students essay exams at least once a semester. These teachers are overlooking a very basic assumption underlying discipline-based writing—that is, the integral part writing plays in learning any subject. When the most frequent use of writing in the disciplines emphasizes only the final product, even that writing is stripped of its usefulness as a medium for teaching and learning.

Clearly, more must be done to train, encourage, and support faculty who are concerned about the state of student writing at UNCW. The first step may be to begin pairing the members of the faculty who expressed interest in team teaching or linking content courses with composition courses to establish a model of this approach. Another important consideration is the kind of publicity the WAC committee generates. Often when a writing-across-the-curriculum program is established, there is much ado quickly fading to very little. Instead of becoming the fabric of the entire university curriculum as it should, the idea nestles comfortably in the pockets of a few departments like an embarrassing piece of lint. Writing a regular column in the student paper, establishing a network among faculty for sharing successes, publishing a newsletter, might be ways to sustain interest. Whatever it takes to shock, shame, or lead our colleagues into the universe of discourse should be our aim.

FACULTY QUESTIONNAIRE RESPONSES

99 responses were received out of 300 surveys.
241 courses are represented.

Responses by Department

English	14	History	3
Creative Arts	12	Math	3
Management	8	Accounting	3
Biology	8	Modern Languages	2
Psychology	8	Military Science	2
Chemistry	6	Political Science	1
Curricular Studies	6	Economics/Finance	1
Sociology/Anthropology	6	Education	1
Philosophy/Religion	5	Nursing	1
HPER	4	Special Programs	1
Earth Science	3	Library	1

Part One

Number of Responses to Each Answered Part of the Questions

1. Student writing on the UNCW campus is
   53 — a serious problem.
   29 — a moderate problem.
   13 — undecided.
   3 — a limited problem.
   1 — not a problem.

2. Regarding the brochure *Writing Across the UNCW Campus*
   37 — I learned new ways to use writing in my courses.
   27 — I learned new techniques.
   34 — I would like a brochure.

3. I use writing in my classes
   68 — as a learning tool.
   71 — as a testing tool.
   30 — as a means to get to know my students better.

4. I would like more information about
   (34 booklets were sent)

5. I would find most helpful
   36 — printed material.
   25 — two-hour workshop.
   10 — a support network.
   5 — mentors.

6. I would be interested in
   24 — team teaching/linking content and composition courses.
   24 — making writing a greater component of my course.
   20 — sharing with the committee a self- or department-developed set of standards for student writing.

Part Two

Writing-Across-the-Curriculum Survey
Instructors were asked to describe the role of writing in their courses.

Rank order of the responses from the second page of the questionnaire. Percentages are of the courses in which writing is a regular part.

93% students informed of the standards
93% feedback is given in organization and style
84% feedback is given according to the adherence to grammatical convention
76% grade depends in part on the quality of writing
76% essay exams
70% out-of-class writing once every two weeks
70% in-class writing less than once every two weeks
56% when writing is required, the students are supplied with models
43% students submit their work in stages
42% write for an audience other than their instructors
40% papers are of 1-4 pages
35% papers are of 5-10 pages
33% writing summaries
31% students may resubmit papers
29% observation logs
26% descriptions
24% no writing component in the course
24% use a peer review process
22% instructor uses a rating sheet for grading
19% almost daily grading outside class
19% almost daily writing in class
19% write about once a week in class
16% lab reports
16% papers are over 10 pages in length
12% microthemes
 7% timed writing
.04% translations

Types of Writing—Rank Order of Frequency

Essay exams	76%	Lab reports	16%
Papers 1-4 pages	40%	Papers of 10 pages	16%
Papers 5-10 pages	35%	Microthemes	12%
Summaries	33%	Timed writing	7%
Observation logs	29%	Translations	.04%
Descriptions	26%		

Writing Centers and the Socratic Ethos

Thomas G. MacLennan

In *The Future of the Humanities*, philosopher Walter Kaufman notes a decline in helping students develop a questioning attitude.[1] The absence of this skill, Kaufman argues, is evident in many areas of higher education. He refers to the propensity for questioning as "the Socratic ethos," and suggests various ways this skill could be revived on college and university campuses. Although Kaufman does not specifically mention writing centers, I think his phrase is an apt credo for the many writing centers that work with promoting writing across the curriculum. This brief report mentions some of the ways The Writing Place, which I direct at UNCW, is working with faculty and students on our campus, promoting the Socratic ethos across the curriculum.

The Writing Place uses a combination of peer and faculty tutors; however, all our tutors practice the Socratic ethos. First, there is the need to effectively prepare tutors to work with students in other disciplines. Most of our peer tutors are students in the Department of English, although we have one tutor with a background in history and journalism. Rather than merely offering prescriptive advice, tutors are trained to be sensitive to what Reigstad and McAndrew call "higher order concerns."[2] They raise questions about how a writer goes about finding a sense of focus, how the piece hangs together, and how the individual parts of the paper are being developed. Tutors frequently ask writers to summarize, or nutshell, parts of the paper. If a writer is stuck, we share brainstorming techniques such as clustering, or free writing. We are finding that these techniques work in all disciplines. All these tutorial approaches raise questions that give writers ownership of their papers.

Although most of the requests we receive come from students completing required papers, writing across the curriculum can be promoted in other writing tasks as well. For example, last semester we helped students complete a variety of writing requests: marine biology scholarship applications, a handicapped student's letter to the editor about accessibility of buildings, several graduate school applications, several résumés and job applications. We even helped a student complete a letter of application for a patent. Students were not our only clientele; we also helped several faculty members in other disciplines raise questions about funding proposals and papers for publication.

In addition to tutoring assistance, we promote the Socratic ethos by working with instructors in demonstrating a variety of ways to incorporate writing into their individual programs. One of our faculty tutors, who is a member of the Writing-Across-the-Curriculum Committee, stresses the need for good writing with a large cross-representation of our faculty. In fact, we have discovered some unusual allies on this committee. Last semester, for example, we worked with an accounting instructor who thinks future accountants should be numerically and syntactically fluent. Together we designed assignments relating to matters of audience, voice, and purpose. Students in his class visited The Writing Place at various stages of composing. We also helped the instructor design an analytic scale to measure growth. Because of our genuine commitment to writing across the curriculum, we believe that writing center personnel must make every effort to work *with* colleagues in exploring the many questions they are raising about assignment design, intervention techniques, and evaluation. These are all legitimate concerns.

In summary, the most important trait a tutor can bring to The Writing Place at UNCW is a questioning attitude. In 1969, Postman and Weingartner eloquently stressed the importance of such an attitude in *Teaching as a Subversive Activity*.[3] At the very heart of their philosophy was a passionate concern that students not only explore the nature of questions, but "generate questions that learners are not, at first, aware of." Indeed, the chapter entitled "What's Worth Knowing?" remains, for me, one of the most vital educational statements I have ever encountered. Whatever term is used—a questions curriculum or the Socratic ethos—the concern for raising and exploring questions should be the essence of any writing center that promotes writing across the curriculum.

References

[1] Walter Kaufman, *The Future of the Humanities* (New York: Thomas Y. Crowell Co., 1977).

[2] Thomas J. Reigstad and Donald A. McAndrew, *Training Tutors for Writing Conferences* (Urbana, Ill.: NCTE, 1984).

[3] Neil Postman and Charles Weingartner, *Teaching as a Subversive Activity* (New York: Dell Publishing Co., 1969).

Writing in a Mathematics Methods Course

Grace Barton

At UNCW I teach courses in mathematics education ranging from the required pre-service courses to a graduate course in diagnosis. My colleagues in composition have convinced me that writing is a way of knowing. As I wish my students to acquire a firm understanding of mathematics curriculum and instruction, incorporating writing makes very good sense to me. With no financial expenditure and little loss of class time, I have made writing an important part of each course.

For several years, I have requested student comments about the course. During the last two years I have made that request formal. Now students are expected to free write for at least five minutes after every class. At the beginning of each class, every student picks up a folder for holding journal writings, reads the comments I have made on the last free write, and deposits the latest entry. The folders are also an efficient way to keep roll, send messages to students, and provide absent students with handouts they missed. Student comments range from objective descriptions of the class to highly subjective condensations of those same 75 minutes. With some students, a continuing conversation emerges early in the semester; others use the journal to vent complaints (which gives me a chance to address them). While students write without self-censorship, they are aware that, if upon rereading they decide the material should not be shared with me, they can staple it closed and place a large red "X" on it. I, of course, respect these signs. From the students' perspective the journals offer a means of personal communication with their instructor and an interesting record of the course.

I also require brief (one- or two-page) reports. Depending upon the course, students assess attainment of conservation, knowledge of the numbers facts, or achievement on standardized or informal instruments, and describe the subject's performance. While the grade for the reports is based on content, I note writing proficiency and students who appear to have deficiencies receive a nonmandatory referral to the campus writing center.

I have also changed assignments that familiarize students with the literature. Formerly, I assigned the summary of a given number of articles. Now I ask students to read several articles and synthesize them in a two-page paper. This assignment more closely approaches my expectation that students will form relationships among topics and requires a level of thinking more appropriate to preprofessionals.

My graduate students complete a major position paper using proper grammatical conventions. As I have come to learn more about the writing process, I have included three new features: focusing the paper on a question rather than a topic, peer review on several preannounced dates, and the use of a rating scale in evaluation. All have increased the quality of the research preceding the writing, as well as the final product.

Students are often required to write essays on examinations. For example, they might be asked to explain a model for a given binary operation or to outline the steps of an algorithm. They also frequently face questions that require both the synthesis of research and good practice and a sensitivity to audience. An example: "Reply to the question 'Why do you use buttons and beans when you teach math?' as posed by a principal, a parent, a janitor, and a student." For the final examination, students have two weeks to answer several questions that require them to make and justify pedagogical decisions, and report the decisions in a variety of written forms such as letters to parents, diagnostic reports, PTA brochures to members, and articles in local papers. I have been pleased with the effects of including more thoughtful writing assignments in my courses, and I will continue to do so in the future.

Writing in a Literature Class
Margaret Parish

"Give me a for instance," a former colleague from South Carolina who once headed our writing center used to say to students. The idea was that the "for instances" made students' writing more concrete and more accessible to the reader.

In one way or another, I am now saying, "Give me a for instance," to students in my literature classes. "Make the most concrete, immediate connection that you can" seems to be what I am asking of them. They might make this connection with expressive writing, or with role play, but it seems important for some of this activity to come before discussion, and surely before their final formulations about the story or poem.

My Introduction to Literature class last semester was almost half a writing class—not critical writing, but writing as a way of knowing, of coming to terms with students' own connectedness with the literature. (There may be an irony in all this writing, considering the fear that some composition theorists express that a *composition* class might turn out to be half *literature* if the camel's nose of poetry

86

and short stories is allowed into the tent.) It is nonetheless true that not only did opportunities for writing keep popping up like crocuses last semester, but other creative activities kept rearing their heads as well. Why? What had changed? Why a decrease of discussion, an increase of creation?

The thrust toward writing across the curriculum on our campus could be part of the explanation. Another reason for this flowering of the written word might lie in the fact that I had team taught in the Cape Fear Writing Project the summer before, thereby gaining new insights from the classroom teachers in our group, especially those from the primary level. What I learned from these teachers seemed to connect with what I had learned earlier, from reading Louise Rosenblatt's *Literature as Exploration* (New York: Noble and Noble, 1968) and from listening to those who had been influenced by her pedagogical philosophy.

I do not want to overemphasize the epiphany aspect of last semester's endeavors. I had surely been using writing in the literature classroom before, but using it primarily in two ways: either I would ask students to predict what was going to happen next in a story and then write about it, or I would stop class discussion when a key issue was raised so that all the students could crystallize their ideas in writing before sharing them with others. I think that much of the writing I was asking from students was analytical rather than creative. I was asking, "What do you think?" more often than, "What do you feel or imagine?" Or even, "What would you do?"

These questions have an important place in a literature classroom, I think, if students are going to "own" what they read there. I conjecture that these questions also have a place in a history class, or in a sociology or political science class as well. The fact that historians often use literature in their teaching probably indicates that they are seeking this sort of immediacy for their students. Writing in response to the literature makes one more connection with events that can sometimes seem remote in time and place.

Remoteness—that was my problem in teaching Richard Wright's "The Man Who Lived Underground" earlier. During one of these efforts, faced with what I considered to be the enormity of the existentialist subtext in the story, I had followed initial class discussion with a brilliant lecture by a visiting philosopher colleague. Starting with Plato's cave, he connected the story in ways that I found fascinating and enlightening. In all honesty, I cannot say that this was true for my students; most of what was said seemed to sail right over their heads—if what they subsequently wrote for me was any indication of their learning experience.

87

This fall I took another approach to teaching the story. In class, students drew the image from the "The Man Who Lived Underground" that was most vivid for them. Then they wrote in their journals about why that particular image was strong for them and how it fit in with other images in the story. In some ways, perhaps, we turned the short story into a film. We went around our circle with each student holding up his or her drawing and talking about it (always with the option of "passing," without which, I believe, no one is going to write uninhibitedly in a journal). Before long, the presenters were interrupted by the voices of other classmates, hypothesizing the significance of the story as a whole. Soon we were launched into a whole class discussion of the story, one in which students consistently connected the meaning they found with their own concrete responses to it.

In teaching *The Lottery*, too, I tried another approach. I once moved too quickly to ask students to connect the story to the "real world." Last semester I asked them to put themselves into the story, to free write about what they would do if they were present when the lottery took place. A class discussion of different possibilities for social change followed, which evolved into two possibilities for final papers. Students could either write about the kinds of social change they would or would not be willing to use to stop the lottery, or they could introduce a new character or characters and change the outcome of the story. Later, when our local paper carried a front-page account of the destruction of a lone Sikh by an angry mob seeking retribution against all Sikhs for the death of Indira Gandhi, students wrote well-focused papers comparing and contrasting that event with *The Lottery*.

The possibilities seem endless. We can never be sure what is going to happen when we ask our students to write and we, in turn, write with them.

STATE UNIVERSITY COLLEGE OF NEW YORK AT FREDONIA

Patrick L. Courts

Improving writing throughout the curriculum and across all disciplines is a major objective of the new General College Program at the State University College of New York at Fredonia. This program, begun in 1983, consists of three major groups of courses: those aimed at developing writing skills; those intended to introduce students to the various disciplines; and integrative, advanced courses intended to help students see relationships among various contents. Although instructors throughout the program are strongly encouraged to include writing activities as an ongoing part of the teaching/learning process, the first part of the program specifically designates "writing-intensive" courses that *must* emphasize writing by including a range of various writing activities. In addition to these "writing-intensive" courses, which may be in any discipline, students are also required to take freshman composition.

The freshman composition course, taught solely by members of the English Department, serves as the foundation for the continuing emphasis on writing throughout the General College Program (GCP). This course resists simplistic "back-to-basics" pressures and engages students in a variety of writing activities, primarily prose, ranging from the personal essay to argument, analysis, and exposition, at the same time it examines the nature and role of language in the students' lives as they extend into the world. In addition to this freshman course, the English Department also offers a range of advanced courses in creative writing, journalism, and professional writing. But the GCP purposely avoids centering all writing instruction in the English Department for several reasons. Because the program genuinely encourages writing instruction in courses throughout the College, students recognize that *writing* and literacy in general are not things isolated in the private worlds of English teachers, but that reading, writing, speaking, and listening are integrated activities of serious importance in all areas. In addition, because the emphasis on writing courses involved in the program is not limited to the freshman year (indeed, many upper-level courses are included), students find themselves involved in writing activities throughout much of their four years at Fredonia.

In addition to taking freshman composition, each student, then, must take at least one writing-intensive course. This may be offered by any department in the College and must meet the following *minimal* requirements: (1) students must write at least three major papers totaling *no less than* 3,500 words, or a series of writing assignments leading to a single paper of no less than 3,500 words; (2) all student writing must be *responded to* and *commented on*, not simply corrected or graded; (3) students must be given the direction and opportunity to rewrite when necessary, constructive, and/or appropriate; (4) each course must be formally approved by a faculty committee that reviews the syllabi and requirements of courses submitted for the writing-intensive part of the Program.

One such intensive course is Media Criticism. This course commits "itself to the investigation of how the media are a shaping force in making humankind become more intellectually and emotionally literate than they presently are. . . . The desired end of the course is 'mediacy'—a term that exists by analogy with 'literacy' and has many similarities to that term." Students are required to keep written journals in which they write a summary or response to daily class activities; a weekly "status report" on their progress in the course; a summary of articles, books, programs, and films that are somehow relevant to the course; and a shot-by-shot analysis of one scene from a ½" videotape per week. In addition to the journal entries, they must also do four "short writing assignments" in which they might, for example, "choose one of the season's new TV shows and (a) explain why and how the program will succeed, (b) review the program, (c) find a professional review of the program and compare it with [their] own, (d) compare/contrast [their] review/analysis of the new program with an established program of 'like' format and content." These assignments are duplicated and used as focal points for small and large group discussions. Finally, students must write a longer paper, which undergoes at least two drafts, that examines the complexities of *television*: that is, what is it? how is it to be 'read'? and what is its purpose?

Although the primary focus of these courses is the specific content of the course (students may even take them in their major area), the writing process must be central to students' mastery of that content and the writing must be viewed both as a means of producing polished, written essays about the content *and* as a heuristic assisting the learner in the understanding of (coming to know) the content. In order to assist faculty in creating and implementing these courses, in addition to improving instruction in general, a faculty development program has been established. This program, consisting of workshops and a series of followup meetings, is designed to involve interested faculty in an exploration of the writing process in general, including peer editing, free writing, ways of responding to student writing, journal writing, conferencing with students about writing activities, and creating writing activities appropriate to a given content area or specific course. Faculty involved in these workshops investigate various approaches to teaching writing, focusing on ideas that have grown out of the work of Moffett, Britton, and others, creating and implementing activities as they make sense with given disciplines.

In all these writing courses, the clear obligation of the instructors is to implement writing activities in the various courses that move beyond the traditional uses of "school writing": more directly, students are not engaged in writing activities simply to produce essays that can be assigned grades. Instructors who agree to implement such courses agree to create writing activities that will actively engage students in using their own language and experiences in order to learn more about the subject matter and about their relationship with that subject matter. Courses presently included in this group cover a broad range of kinds of writing, using everything from the traditional research paper to fictional accounts of anthropological expeditions.

Finally, the various writing courses resist the idea that words and language are simply tools. At Fredonia we believe that language and the written word are liberating instruments as the individual attempts to live and learn in the world, that the composing process is an essential element in coming to know oneself and one's relationship with and among others in the world. Thus it is that the first writing courses of the General College Program address the general issue of literacy, attempting to counteract the development of surrogate, utilitarian, and technical sublanguages and subvert the notion of literacy as a rigid and limiting skill. Literacy is always more than mere propriety and good usage, matters that are more imitative than liberating—as important as most matters of propriety, but no more important. The ability to manipulate, to "use," and to know in and through written (and spoken) language is the basic requirement of the creation and communication of knowledge. Learning to speak, to write, and to compose is the means by which a person creates, discovers, and externalizes what s/he knows. It is coextensive with the knowing process.

91

THE UNIVERSITY OF MICHIGAN
Patricia L. Stock

Based in contemporary theories of learning, the writing program at The University of Michigan focuses both on the power of writing as a way of learning and the activities of reading and writing as socialization into disciplinary communities. James B. White, Professor of Law, English Language and Literature, and Classics at The University of Michigan, illustrates the philosophy and practice of this approach when he describes how he teaches law by teaching writing and writing by teaching law:

> . . . [L]iteracy is not merely the capacity to understand the conceptual content of writing and utterances, but the ability to participate fully in a set of social and intellectual practices. It is not passive but active . . . for participation in the speaking and writing of language is participation in the activities it makes possible. Indeed it involves a perpetual remaking both of language and of practice.[1]

When he teaches law, White asks students to draft rules of their own devising with materials from their own lives so that the process seems "natural and immediate" to them, and so that they learn the limits of language and mind. In the process, White believes students will be introduced

> to questions . . . about the construction of social reality through language (as they define roles, voices, and characters in the dramas they report); about the definition of value (as they find themselves talking about privacy or integrity or truthfulness or cooperation); about the nature of reasoning (as they put forward one or another argument with the expectation that it cannot be answered, as they try to meet the argument of another, and so on). (p. 57)

When writing across the curriculum is thus conceived as a means of inviting students to become full participants in the law, or chemistry, or women's studies, it cannot be prepackaged into textbooks for students or handbooks for teachers or administrators. Such a program requires that an entire faculty introduce into professional conversations the issues implicit in teaching and learning the discourse systems of the academy and, in many cases, of the marketplace. The faculty of Michigan's College of Literaure, Science, and the Arts (LS&A) chose to do that by (1) constituting an English Composition Board (ECB), composed of six faculty members, two from the Department of English and four from other departments or programs within the College, to be an agent of the College faculty, "responsible to every unit in the College but the responsibility of none";[2] and by (2) charging the Board with developing and overseeing the writing program which was adopted in the College in 1978 and subsequently by most other units in the University. The work of the Board, funded by the Andrew W. Mellon Foundation for the 1978-79 academic year and by the University since that time, has seven parts, six within the University, and one beyond its boundaries. The responsibilities within the University are these:

1. *Administration of an entrance essay required of all incoming undergraduates.* During an orientation session, students who newly enter the University write for 50 minutes on a subject of general knowledge. Two experienced teachers of composition evaluate each essay holistically. If the two readers fail to agree about the quality of the essay, a third resolves the disagreement. Based upon this evaluation, students are placed in tutorial composition classes or introductory composition classes, or are exempted from taking any entrance-level writing course.

2. *Tutorial composition instruction required of all students who demonstrate on the entrance essay that they need such assistance.* In tutorial composition classes, no more than 16 students receive concentrated instruction in writing from experienced, full-time composition teachers who constitute the faculty of the ECB. Tutorial classes meet together for four hours each week and students in those classes meet individually with their teachers for at least one half-hour a week. At the end of seven weeks, tutorial students who demonstrate sufficient growth as writers in a posttest examination move on to introductory composition or are exempted from any further introductory-level instruction.

3. *Introductory composition required of most students to make them more proficient writers.* Students may fulfill the introductory composition requirement by completing one of several courses. Most students elect to take English 125 (Introductory Composition) taught in the English Department primarily by Graduate Student Teaching Assistants (GSTAs); this course requires students to write for a variety of audiences, purposes, and occasions. Other students fulfill the requirement by taking an introductory course in Shakespeare, taught in the English Department; Great Books, taught within the Honors Program; College Thinking, taught as a University course; or a freshman seminar, taught in the Residential College in any area and based on any subject the faculty choose.

93

4. *Writing Workshop support available to every student.* Students are entitled to the support of experienced teachers of composition at any stage of their own work to compose a piece of writing for any course.

5. *Junior/Senior level writing courses offered and required primarily in students' areas of concentration.* Junior/Senior writing courses are taught in all departments, with the exception of some few departments such as far eastern languages, by regular members of the faculty, many of whom are assisted by GSTAs. More than 170 such courses are taught each year. In each junior/senior level writing course the substance of the course is its subject matter; writing functions not only as a vehicle for communication but also for learning. In all cases, regular faculty members read and evaluate students' writing.

6. *Research into the effectiveness of all parts of the program.* In research reported by Richard W. Bailey, Professor of English Language and Literature at The University of Michigan, the effectiveness of the entrance essay as an indicator of students' ability to succeed at the University and of the writing program as a whole is demonstrated.[3]

The seventh part of Michigan's writing program includes activities relating the teaching of writing at the University to the teaching of writing in secondary schools, community colleges, and other colleges and universities. These activities include the following:

- *Writing conferences* at the University intended primarily to inform teachers of the ECB's program of instruction, and on an ongoing basis, what it is learning about the teaching of writing.

- *One-day and two-day seminars* conducted in secondary schools, community colleges, and universities throughout the state of Michigan and beyond, designed to familiarize entire faculties with the University's writing program and to discuss with teachers the current state of theory and practice in the art of teaching writing at all levels.

- *Writing workshops*, held at the University each summer, designed to provide teachers with intensive work in the teaching of writing.

- *Extended curriculum and staff-development projects* for school districts and universities that have requested such service.

- Publication from 1979 to 1982 of *Fforum*, a journal providing teachers of writing at all levels of instruction with a place for mutual instruction and dialogue. Over 50 essays originally published in *Fforum* have been expanded into a book.[4]

The University of Michigan's outreach program testifies to the fact that Michigan faculty believe an effective writing program must be as sensitive to students' past experiences as writers as it is to those experiences it predicts students must anticipate in their future. It is for this reason that Michigan faculty have so energetically invited their colleagues at all levels of instruction throughout the state of Michigan to join them in their conversations about the teaching of writing.

References

[1] J. B. White, "The Invisible Discourse of the Law: Reflections on Legal Literacy and General Education," in *Fforum*, ed. P. L. Stock, pp. 46-59 (Upper Montclair, N.J.: Boynton Cook, 1983).

[2] Minutes of the 16 January 1978 Faculty Meeting of the College of Literature, Science, and the Arts, The University of Michigan.

[3] R. W. Bailey, "This Teaching Works: The English Composition Board at The University of Michigan." Report to the Regents, 1981.

[4] P. L. Stock, ed., *Fforum: Essays in Theory and Practice in the Teaching of Writing* (Upper Montclair, N.J.: Boynton Cook, 1983).

MONTANA STATE UNIVERSITY
Mark L. Waldo

Montana State University's cross-curriculum writing project began in earnest in 1980 when members of the English Department applied for and received a major grant from the Fund for Improvement of Post-Secondary Education (FIPSE). The grant funded a series of writing workshops for selected faculty and staff from every academic division on campus. Out of these workshops grew a variety of sound and attractive techniques for instituting writing in the content areas. And out of them has evolved a sophisticated and comprehensive support system for composition: MSU's Writing Center, which assumed responsibility for the university-wide writing program two years ago.

The degree of success we have achieved is attributable primarily to three aspects of our program. First, our upper administration is supportive without being impositional. The office of Academic Vice President is particularly enthusiastic about our cross-curriculum effort. All admininstrators have used numerous public contexts to applaud competent writing as an essential goal of university education. They have also taken more substantive steps, from funding the Writing Center to providing financial incentives to faculty, in order to improve the climate for teaching writing. And yet none of them would, even if such a step were possible, force writing into every course. We emphasize voluntary faculty action in each of our projects. MSU began with a small but dedicated group of faculty advocates for writing. Along with the Writing Center's consultants, these advocates have worked with their interested colleagues in bringing writing to courses ready for it. Now, more than a third of MSU's faculty requires writing on a regular basis.

Second, our cross-curricular program is successful because we have helped faculty develop an attractive package of assignment options, including unevaluated journal writing and short pieces of shaped writing designed to enhance learning and thinking skills. The structure and goals for these latter assignments, sometimes called microthemes, are determined mainly by the instructors themselves. As a consequence, they tend to fit snugly into the intellectual and pedagogical fabric of a course; they are also easy to explain to students through modeling and efficient to evaluate through holistic score sheets, criteria sheets, or brief commentary.

A good illustration is the case of economics Professor P. J. Hill, who added short essay assignments to a sophomore-level course he taught in the fall quarter of 1984. He had never before required any writing in this course because he thought it was too large and unwieldy, enrolling more than 80 students. What kind of assignments could he give to that number and how could he grade them? His experience with bringing writing to Econ 278 reflects the merit of a program that relies upon advocacy. Two of Hill's colleagues in the Economics Department described their successes with the use of short, goal-oriented essays in their own large classes. They also brainstormed with him about potential topics for his papers. By the time Hill sought out Writing Center personnel for help with assignment design and evaluation, he had already listened to the testimony of firm believers and had himself composed 60 situational assignments that suited the context of his course.

Three of Hill's assignments are as follows:

1. You are enrolled in an art history class at Montana State in which the instructor says that Michelangelo's *Pieta* is a "priceless" work of art. You note that, in terms of your economics class, this has certain implications about the demand curve for the *Pieta*. Write a short essay to your instructor, using the concept of demand to comment on her statement.

2. A few years ago, McDonald's started opening earlier and serving breakfast. One friend says that this is just another example of the greed of large corporations: "They weren't satisfied with the profits they already had—instead they wanted to make even more." Another friend disagreed: "It was an effort to make the customers happy—most fast food restaurants don't serve breakfast; in doing so McDonald's is performing a real service for the people who want a quick, reasonably priced breakfast." Who is correct? Write a short essay to your friends that will help them solve this disagreement.

3. A wealthy individual buys a thousand acres of land adjacent to Gallatin Field (Bozeman's airport). He plans to raise registered quarter horses. Two years later he sues the airport authority, claiming that noise from planes is making his horses nervous, significantly reducing their value and consequently lessening his income. You are the District Court judge who hears the suit. Using the economic approach to pollution, write a brief summary of your ruling and the reasons for it.

Such assignments promote learning and thinking, at the same time giving students a sense of purpose and audience for their writing. All the Center's consultants had to do, then, was suggest some shapes for the writing, describe how models might aid students in their approach to each assignment, and help design a useful scoring instrument. (A generic scale for assessing "Thesis-Support Microthemes'' in Finance follows.) Each of Hill's students was required to write on any six of the 60 topics, with due dates spaced throughout the quarter. Scoring a set of essays took no more time, he found, than scoring a batch of the multiple-choice exams he had previously used. And the writing augmented learning much more effectively. Because of his success, Hill is now a vocal advocate of composition in classes both large and small.

Not all our experiences proceed with the hitchless ease of the P. J. Hill episode. But we have had no failures. If lack of failures is attributable, first, to the program's philosophy of collaboration with *willing* faculty and, second, to the comparative attractiveness of the writing package we have to offer, there is a third aspect of our program that generates cross-curricular good will: the MSU Writing Center. From its inception the Center was designed to be ambitious. It provides experienced consultants to faculty such as P. J. Hill who wish to bring writing into classes but do not wish to be buried under the paperweight of grading. And it offers tutoring help to students writing papers for any of their courses.

Our Writing Center is far from the comma clinic or grammar garage that has characteristically been the English Skills Lab of the past. It is an energizing place, full of the low hum of talk about issues that matter to students as they compose. Twenty-five trained student tutors (undergraduates of varying majors), four instructional tutors (all with B.A.s or M.A.s and extensive experience teaching and tutoring writing), and four faculty writing consultants (who are also instructors in the freshman writing program) work toward the common goal of enhancing the thinking and writing abilities of those who visit. Center personnel will work with students on any phase of the composing process, from discovering topics and generating ideas to developing and organizing supporting materials through styling and editing final drafts. Two things that Center personnel will not do: they will not write papers for students—instead they use the inquiry method to get students to do the writing; and they will not pull out exercise workbooks to teach students about comma splices or dangling modifiers. Our intention is to make the Writing Center the compositional heart of the institution; and with 5,500 visitations in its first year from faculty, undergraduate and graduate students from every department on campus, we believe we have a good start toward achieving that goal.

In addition to offering students almost unlimited opportunity for feedback on papers, the Writing Center promotes the cross-curriculum effort in other ways. It relieves the burden some faculty feel of dealing with ''hordes of students'' who want their papers read in

PRIMARY TRAIT ANALYTIC SCALE FOR "THESIS-SUPPORT MICROTHEMES" IN FINANCE
(P. J. Hill)

There are various degrees of quality of support. Immediately coming to mind are the following: empirical evidence, theoretical argument, authority, and intuition. These types of support have values as they are listed. That is to say, empirical evidence weighs stronger than theoretical argument, which weighs stronger than authority, etc. When using different types of support, students should take into account such factors as the following:

For empirical evidence:
  a. the past versus the future
  b. precise pertinence of the data to the thesis
  c. the unbiased or biased nature of the data.

For authority:
  a. the past record of the authority
  b. qualifications of the authority
  c. the extent of concurrence with other authorities.

Thesis-support microthemes should be written so that they are clear to persons who are not members of the class or who are not even business majors. They should not be written so that they can be understood only if the reader already knows the thesis and its support. In other words, the thesis supports must be complete and sufficient.

GRADING CRITERIA

Support of Theses	Other Feedback
A. CLARITY OF SUPPORT _____ (0-5 scale)	Grammatical errors are numerous enough to interfere with understanding your response. ( )
B. LOGIC: (Relationship of support to thesis) _____	The organization of your response is not clear.( )
C. SOURCES OF SUPPORT	
1. Quantity _____	The logic of your support is confusing or does not make sense. ( )
2. Quality _____	Your conclusions are not warranted by your support. ( )
TOTAL MICROTHEME GRADE _____	Your support is too imprecise or too general. ( )

advance of the due date. I realize that most readers will immediately say that faculty should *want* to look at their students' papers anytime, perhaps particularly in advance of the due date. I agree that they should. Nonetheless, a few instructors view conferences on rough drafts as part of the "working baggage" of writing—the additional effort required if one is to add composition to a class. Other instructors may lack confidence in dealing with the drafts of their students. Our Writing Center lessens a bit of the angst felt by each of those groups. The Center also sponsors and directs a variety of experimental projects to determine what effect increased writing activity is having on our students' thinking and writing skills. We have abundant testimony that the results are quite positive, but empirical evidence is slower in coming.

In my view, our program is integrative and organic, each aspect supporting and nourishing the others. Our continued effectiveness depends upon the nondictatorial support of the administration, the willingness of the faculty to share their successes with their colleagues, and the expansion of the Writing Center as a comprehensive support system for composition. At present, I am very optimistic about the further growth of the writing program at Montana State.

7. Faculty Workshops

Faculty workshops and programs in writing across the curriculum have been described in a number of journal articles (102, 5, 83, 37, 20). This chapter presents brief lesson plans for a series of workshops that draw on my reading of these writers, ideas presented in previous chapters, and my own experiences conducting content writing workshops on a number of campuses. I do not imagine or intend that faculties anywhere will take these lessons as a script and use them unmodified in efforts to develop cross-campus writing programs. At the same time, I believe the topics dealt with in these workshops are fundamental for faculty groups seriously interested in coming to grips with the writing crisis.

My workshops are divided into two groups: the Writing Workshops (designated W-1, W-2, etc.) and the Teaching Workshops (T-1, T-2, etc.). The Writing Workshops are dedicated to the principle—now axiomatic in the writing profession—that teachers of writing should experience the process of composition both as they teach it and as they talk about teaching it. The Writing Workshops, then, are a series of writing activities that I have used with faculty groups of mixed disciplines. The "assignments" are designed to elicit impromptu writing (except for W-6, which involves a sustained piece of writing based on outside research).

The Teaching Workshops follow the chapter order of this monograph and lead groups in examining key issues. A consistent focus in these workshops is on helping content teachers make applications to their own classrooms. Indeed, I think it is essential to the success of any writing-across-the-curriculum project that from the start faculty members commit themselves to assigning and collecting student writing in their classes in order to use it as a source of material for discussion.

The Writing and Teaching workshops can often be mixed in seminars and workshops. I generally begin a session with one of the Writing Workshops, allowing, say, an hour or more for writing and discussion of writing. Then groups move into one of the Teaching Workshops for discussion of pedagogy. Although the numbers imply a six- (or twelve-) session program, these workshops have been conducted in as little as a single intensive weekend.

INTERDISCIPLINARY NONTRIVIAL PURSUIT

OVERVIEW

This workshop engages content and English instructors in describing what they see as important in their disciplines and making connections between language use and knowing in the disciplines. It involves very little writing; it serves as a nonthreatening introductory activity.

MATERIALS

Index cards or slips of paper, two per participant.

PROCEDURES

This is a trivia game that pits the members of the workshop against Demon Ignorance.

Participants pair off, and each pair collaborates in writing four questions (and answers). Each question is to center on the pair's view of a significant or important piece of knowledge in the following areas:

1. Humanities and arts
2. Mathematics and science
3. Applied arts and sciences (business, law, technology)
4. Wild card (or any area not covered by 1-3).

Each pair also rates the difficulty level of each question on a scale of 1 (quite easy, common knowledge) to 10 (a difficult question, answer not widely known).

The leader collects the cards and reads the questions aloud. Workshop participants try to answer the questions (writers, naturally, may not answer their own questions). When the group answers correctly, it receives the difficulty level (1-10) in points. When the group cannot answer a question, Demon Ignorance gets the points. The rating system is designed to make the contest a close one: a single missed difficult question can give Ignorance more points than several easy correct answers. The game is played until the questions have been exhausted and, one hopes, Ignorance has been put to flight.

DISCUSSION

The following questions help the group zero in on the connections between language and learning:

1. Why did various pairs identify certain aspects of knowledge as "important"? What were their criteria? How do opinions of relative importance vary within the group?

2. How much of commonly held knowledge is a matter of direct personal experience? (Who has *seen* William Shakespeare or an electron?) How much of our knowledge is carried to us by language (by a kind of scholarly hearsay)?

3. What sorts of semantic disputes and quibbles arose during the game? Did some "right" answers turn out to be "it all depends on what you mean"?

4. What did people learn from the game? about the world? about language?

FOLLOWUP

The group can discuss how language functions as a carrier of learning in various disciplines. What are the unique language problems in chemistry? physics? business? architecture? English?

HOW THINGS CHANGE

OVERVIEW

This workshop involves informal historical writing as participants compare two eras. It also encourages content teachers to explore the relationship between personal experience and good writing.

PROCEDURES

Each participant writes two stories or descriptions, one about life during his/her youth, one about life now. Possible topics for comparison are

Food	Parenting
Television	Money
School	Leisure
Teaching	Possessions
Cars	Jobs
Sports	Death
Politics	Religion
Sex roles	Ethics
War	

The old maxim "Show, don't tell" operates here. Writers are to tell stories rather than offering generalizations. Only after writers have composed their two stories are they allowed to write a generalization or two about "How Things Change." The workshop leader should stress that these writings will be shared informally and that they will be treated as drafts, not polished copy. If the workshop group is large, pairs of writers can read their work to one another. In most workshops public readings of these personal histories will be quite satisfying and will launch the group on a nostalgia trip.

DISCUSSION

1. Is this history? (Opinions will differ.)
2. Are the generalizations valid?
3. How did storytelling generate material for the generalizations?
4. What difficulties did writers have in getting started? How can a teacher provide prewriting assistance to students?

5. How pleasant or unpleasant was the sharing of writing? Where does the bashfulness and even apprehension come from? What are the implications for teaching writing?

FOLLOWUP

A common problem in having students write in history (and in other subjects) is their tendency to write abstract generalizations, frequently gleaned from the textbook. This storytelling approach to history writing lets students bring personal experience to bear on the generalizations they make. How can the approach be extended to other disciplines?

HEY RUBE!

OVERVIEW

This workshop has people invent and explain wonderful gadgets to make life better for humankind. It helps participants explore some aspects of technical writing.

RESOURCE

(Optional) *The Best of Rube Goldberg*, compiled by Charles Keller (Englewood Cliffs, N.J.: Prentice-Hall, 1979).

PROCEDURES

Almost everyone knows of the cartoonist Rube Goldberg and his curiously complex contraptions like the Automatic Weight-Reducing Machine, and Self-Emptying Ashtrays. Each device consisted of a succession of levers, pulleys, springs, strings, and gears to transfer motion and achieve the desired effect. If the leader has the Keller book available, participants can enjoy studying how Goldberg would Keep the Baby Covered at Night or Put Postage Stamps on Envelopes. Goldberg presented diagrams of his devices, then offered an explanation. This writing experiment reverses that order:

1. The group can brainstorm for desperately needed devices (such as Goldberg's Simple Way to Open an Egg, Self-Working Tire Pump, Mosquito Bite Scratcher, or Self-Operating Napkin).

2. Each person writes a description of how one such device would work. Part of the fun is to make the device as complex and circuitous as possible. The rhetorical aim, however, remains clarity of expression for an audience.

3. (Optional) The writer may create a diagram of his/her device.

Writing and diagrams are shared. The group may grant awards for best idea, worst idea, most impractical idea, and best-written description.

DISCUSSION

1. What obstacles did people encounter in trying to describe their devices in writing?

2. Were there problems in comprehending the written descriptions? Did the writers anticipate these problems?

3. In what ways does making a diagram simplify the writing task? Are pictures worth a thousand words? In what ways are words more helpful than pictures?

4. What sorts of "technical" writing do students do in their various university courses? What sort of advice and assistance can the content teacher give them in process to make their writing more articulate and precise?

FOLLOWUP

The leader (or a faculty member in the technical fields) might bring in several samples of popular and academic technical writing, ranging from instructions on how to assemble a bicycle to a maintenance manual for a laboratory apparatus. The workshop members can discuss the quality of these writings and ways in which technical writing by professionals can be improved.

W-4
WHAT'S NEW?

OVERVIEW

In this workshop, faculty members select a key or current concept in their discipine and write about it for two different audiences.

PROCEDURES

Each participant selects an important new idea in his/her discipline. To warm up for writing, the scholar creates some writer-based prose, describing the idea for him/herself. What is the idea? What is my grasp of it? How do I feel about this idea? Does it upset any of my preconceived notions?

Then each person creates two pieces of public or reader-based writing:

1. A memorandum to a colleague in the *same discipline* describing some aspect of the idea or rendering a professional opinion about its value or worth. (The colleague may be a participant.)

2. A memorandum or note to someone in another discipline explaining the idea. Again a participant—presumably from a different college or division—can serve as audience.

Participants can share and discuss the writing, with the readers raising any questions they have about the concept and/or the writing.

DISCUSSION

1. In what ways does writer-based or personal or journal-style writing help one clarify ideas? (Even professionals sometimes need to clarify their knowledge; journals are not just for students.)

2. What factors entered into your writing a memo to a colleague in the same field? Which of these were centered in the subject matter? Which were human problems of communicating with an expert and a colleague?

3. How did writing for the nonspecialist differ?

FOLLOWUP

This activity can generate very useful discussions of the value of different audiences for student writing. The leader can help the group develop a sense of some of the alternative audiences for writing, both on campus and off.

A GUIDE TO THE INSTITUTION

OVERVIEW

In this workshop, participants write an insider's guide to their department, unit, or college to explore how personal knowledge affects style and content in writing.

RESOURCES

Several copies of the current college or university catalog and/or promotional or descriptive literature about the institution.

PROCEDURES

The leader can begin by reading (or having participants read) some of the published descriptions of the institution, perhaps beginning with the president's introduction and leading to the statements of rules and requirements for various departments. Such readings often prompt mutterings among college faculty, because everyone recognizes that the reality of campus life differs from the descriptions. The leader then invites people to write brief "insider's guides" to the place. Among the options:

- A letter to entering freshmen suggesting what they should "really" look for and "really" do to acclimate themselves.
- A guide to the prospective major outlining the ins and outs of the department.
- A brochure for prospective faculty members listing the unpublished advantages and disadvantages of faculty life.
- An insider's guide to the _____ department.
- A flowchart or checklist for getting ideas and proposals through the academic governance system.

The products of this writing session generally make good and amusing sharing.

DISCUSSION

1. How does your personal knowledge of the institution affect your writing of these guides?
2. What are the analogous forms of "insider's knowledge" in the field or discipline? For example, what do experienced automotive engineers or musicians know about their fields that allows

for shortcuts in seeking knowledge and helps them write successfully?

3. Is writing in the disciplines objective? In what ways? In what ways is it subjective, even when it appears objective?

4. Why are college catalogs written as they are written? Why are scholarly articles written as *they* are written? Why is inside knowledge generally excluded from such publications?

5. Do students write as insiders or outsiders on content matters? Should that be changed?

FOLLOWUP

The writings that emerge in this session are probably not the sort of thing the college would publish—they tell too much. Participants might find it profitable to rewrite their pieces into forms that keep the essential insider's information but present a tone or image more in keeping with traditional university publications.

QUESTING

OVERVIEW

The five previous Writing Workshops generally call for impromptu writing that allows participants to draw on existing knowledge. It is also useful for faculty members to carry at least one piece of writing through the writing process—selecting a topic, doing research, drafting a paper, revising it in groups, and presenting final, polished copy. Questing engages the workshop participants in writing full-fledged papers on a common theme or topic.

RESOURCE

Participants should read the description of "The Quest Program" in Chapter 5, pp. 63–66.

PROCEDURES

The faculty group chooses a broad topic of interest to all members and plans to investigate it thoroughly, with each member taking responsibility for researching and writing about one aspect. The topic should be broad enough to be of interest to faculty in both the sciences and the humanities. A helpful technique is for the leader to bring in a daily newspaper or a weekly newsmagazine and to have the group study it for possible topics. A useful pattern for the Quest follows.

Session One. The group selects a topic. Members develop a list of key questions or topics to be investigated. Individuals commit themselves to working on one part of the topic. They discuss resources: Where can we go to find anwers?

Session Two. Participants gather and analyze data. They read and research and come to the workshop prepared to discuss their findings with others in the group. They consider the writing: How can this information be conveyed most effectively to a larger audience? They do preliminary planning (prewriting) of papers.

Session Three. Drafts are due. Participants meet in small groups to experience peer editing.

Session Four. Participants bring final copies of their papers to the workshop to be be shared, appreciated, and assessed.

DISCUSSION

Participants should discuss their experiences at each stage of the Quest. (It is useful for them to end each session with a brief free write summing up their impressions and conclusions, both about the Quest and the implications for teaching writing in the content areas.) At the conclusion, they should review the entire writing process and make connections with writing projects in their own fields.

WRITING AS A WAY OF KNOWING

OVERVIEW

This workshop introduces a series of teaching workshops. It combines well with W-1, "Interdisciplinary Nontrivial Pursuit," which can function as an icebreaker as well as raising some significant questions about writing.

RESOURCES

Chapter 1. Ideally, participants will have read this chapter before the session. Alternatively, the workshop leader can either summarize it or, better, present his/her own view of content writing.

(Optional) Read and discuss samples of student writing that participants bring with them. (Considerable prior notice may be needed for this. In announcing the workshops, the leader might ask content teachers to begin saving writing.)

PROCEDURES

In contrast to the Writing Workshops, outlined previously, there is no step-by-step procedure for the Teaching Workshops; they will vary considerably with the needs of the group and the interests of the leader. At initial workshop sessions I try to accomplish the following:

- Provide an overview of the idea of content writing, where it comes from, why it is a current issue.
- Reassure content teachers that this whole notion does not necessarily mean a great deal of work; if content writing is to be viable in their courses, it must pay its own way in improved learning.
- Examine some student writing. What is good and bad about the way our students write? (I usually rule out discussion of grammar, spelling, mechanics in the early stages of this discussion. The focus should be on how students handle or mishandle content.)
- Outline a set of aims or expectations for the workshop. What will content teachers get from it? What will be expected of them?

FOLLOWUP

Each participant should, if at all possible, make a commitment to do some writing instruction in his/her course and to share the results with the group. If funds/time/energies permit, the leader might make a commitment to visit the classes of interested participants to observe the content being taught and make suggestions about incorporating writing.

WORKADAY WRITING

OVERVIEW

This workshop shows how writing can be worked into many courses on an almost regular basis, with emphasis on writing that is helpful to the student but does not require elaborate commentary by the instructor.

RESOURCES

Chapter 2.

Samples of workaday writing brought in by workshop participants—"throwaway" writing in the form of notes, memos, letters, etc., that they use in their everyday teaching and research.

PROCEDURES

- Review the broad concept of workaday writing: it is generally writer-based rather than reader-based; it functions more as a means of data gathering and analysis than as a way of communicating findings; it requires little or no instructor commentary.
- Review the list of writing forms provided in Figure 1, page 26.
- Have participants suggest additional workaday writing forms, the daily writing they do in their work.
- Have participants work in pairs or small groups divided by disciplines. (If available, English department members knowledgeable about content writing can be assigned as consultants or advisors to each group.) In groups, participants brainstorm for ways of adding more workaday writing to their courses.

FOLLOWUP

Each participant (including English department members) agrees to elicit some workaday writing from one or more classes before the next workshop session, in which time is given to discussing and analyzing what happened and the quality of writing that emerged.

WRITING ASSIGNMENTS IN THE CONTENT AREAS

OVERVIEW

Participants discuss the qualities of a good writing assignment or project and develop a specific activity for one of their classes.

RESOURCES

Chapter 3, pp. 30–35 ("Assignment Making"), Chapter 5; copies of Figure 2, p. 32.

Prior planning: Participants should come with the necessary materials to write a content-specific assignment for one of their courses.

PROCEDURES

The leader might begin by eliciting from participants a list of general criteria for good assignments in college. What do you have to tell students? How do people present assignments and projects? What sorts of constraints, deadlines, due dates are required?

Following up on the material presented in this monograph, the leader can then suggest that good writing assignments are vital, that much poor student writing can be traced directly to writing activities that merely call for regurgitation of information.

After ample discussion, the leader can have participants prepare specific writing assignments for their current or future courses, following the procedure outlined in the monograph (or adapted to fit the experience and needs of the participants and leader). Assignments should be shared and discussed, with members of the group proposing additional ideas for one another's assignments.

FOLLOWUP

Naturally, the leader hopes participants will test these assignments in their own classes. The two subsequent workshops provide for further development of the activity and for assessment of results.

THE WRITING PROCESS IN THE CONTENT AREAS

OVERVIEW

Working with the assignments created in workshop T-3, participants plan activities for planning and writing, with an emphasis on using content expertise to guide students to successful papers.

RESOURCES

Chapter 3, pp. 35–38 and pp. 43–45 (''Preparation for Writing'' and ''Writing'').

Assignments from Workshop T-3.

PROCEDURES

The leader can begin by stressing that the process of writing in the content areas should be guided by the subject-matter specialist's understanding of the discipline, that he or he is a teacher of writing through the content of the course.

After reviewing the concepts covered in Chapter 3, participants should work on planning specific activities to implement a content writing assignment. They should list as many activities and possibilities as they can. *Overkill* is the word; they should plan more activities than they would ever use. As group members share their ideas, individual instructors can pare down their plans to workable dimensions.

FOLLOWUP

Many of the participants should now be ready to begin teaching the assignment in their classes. Ideally, they will bring drafts of student writing to Workshop T-5.

REVISING AND ASSESSMENT

OVERVIEW

Participants continue to develop ideas for a writing project in the content areas, creating activities for revision and proofreading, sharing, and student and instructor assessment.

RESOURCES

Chapter 3, pp. 45–50, ("Revising," "Proofreading," and "Presenting"); Chapter 4.

PROCEDURES

This workshop is potentially the most difficult and possibly explosive in a writing-across-the-curriculum seminar. Notions and biases about "good English" and correctness run deep in the minds of nonspecialists and English instructors alike. Time must be taken to discuss a philosophy of assessment clearly and carefully.

The philosophy presented in this monograph is that content instructors should focus attention primarily on content-related problems and errors. Whether or not they subscribe to that philosophy, content instructors should be warned about the dangers of harsh red-penciling of student writing. The leader might find it useful to have participants clarify their thinking about correctness, evaluation, and assessment through a workaday free writing to be shared with the class.

If some members of the group have made their assignments to their classes and collected some drafts, this would be a good time to look at them and to consider ways in which assessment and evaluation can be made productive for the students.

Finally, the question of grading will undoubtedly emerge and it should be given ample time. The philosophy espoused in this monograph is, predictably, content-centered, suggesting that writing quality be insisted upon but not necessarily folded into a grade. Many participants will disagree with that philosophy, and the leader may want to have other grading schemes in mind to share with the group.

FOLLOWUP

When most instructors in the group have been through a major writing project with their students, the seminar can reconvene for discussion. Samples of finished student writing can be displayed and discussed. The key question to be discussed here is, "In what ways does the writing enhance learning in the disciplines?" Candid responses should be invited. The leader should also be prepared to help content specialists inexperienced in responding to student writing see the ways in which learning is demonstrated and develop ways of responding to it.

A WRITING POLICY ACROSS THE CURRICULUM

OVERVIEW

This workshop is both an end and a beginning. Having developed some expertise in teaching writing in the content areas, participants move from discussions of individual teaching to college or university policy.

RESOURCE

Chapter 6.

PROCEDURES

These will vary widely from one college to another and will depend on the makeup of the group, resources and administrative support, and the perception of the urgency of the writing problem.

In conducting such discussions, I have always proceeded with three broad questions:

1. *What is the responsibility of the English department in the teaching of writing?* The nature of the required English course will invariably come up here. It is my belief that English departments should focus on developing comfort with the writing process, broad fluency, and a reasonable degree of mechanical accuracy. They should also include some content writing in their courses (more than the usual "research paper"). English departments cannot and should not, however, try to teach discipline-specific writing skills; that is clearly the province of the content instructor.

2. *What is the responsibility of content departments?* My view is that subject-matter departments ought to develop the specific writing skills required in their disciplines, linking writing with ways of learning in the field. Each department may seek alternative ways to to this. Should writing be required in *all* content courses? Can/Should writing-intensive courses be designed by the content faculty who like to teach writing? Should there be incentives for content faculty members to teach writing?

3. *What is our policy?* Given resources, personnel, the nature of the student body, and all the other variables and intangibles, what is our policy? This is a most difficult writing "assignment," and may lead to many additional workshops or to subcommittee writing. Frequently research into the institution will be required. A solid, articulate writing policy statement, however, is, to my mind, a necessary outcome of this workshop.

FOLLOWUP

Fourth and fifth questions may also be taken up:

4. *How do we articulate our policy to our students?*
5. *How do we articulate our policy to "feeder" secondary schools?*

Bibliography

1. Abrams, Kathleen. "Literature and Science: An Interdisciplinary Approach to Environmental Studies." *Current Review* 18 (October 1979): 302-4.

2. Adams, James L. *Conceptual Blockbusters*. New York: W.H. Freeman, 1974.

3. Barrow, Lloyd H., and Salesi, Rosemary. "Integrating Science Activities Through Literature Webs." *School Science and Mathematics* 82 (January 1982): 65-70.

4. Beck, James. "Theory and Practice of Interdisciplinary English." *English Journal* 69 (February 1979): 28-32.

5. Behrens, Laurence. "Writing, Reading, and the Rest of the Faculty." *English Journal* 67 (September 1978): 54-60.

6. Beyer, Barry K. "Pre-writing and Rewriting to Learn." *Social Education* 43 (March 1979): 187-89, 197.

7. _____, and Brostoff, Anita. "The Time It Takes: Managing/Evaluating Writing and Social Studies." *Social Education* 43 (March 1979): 194-97.

8. Blaya, Jeffrey J. "Say Good-Bye to Those Dumb Old Term Papers." *AV Instructor* 22 (June–July 1977): 16-18.

9. Botein, Stephen, and others, eds. *Experiments in History Teaching*. Cambridge, Mass.: Harvard University, Danforth Center, 1977.

10. Bredderman, Ted. "What Research Says: Activity Science—the Evidence Shows It Matters." *Science and Children* 20 (September 1982): 39-41.

11. Britton, James et al. *The Development of Writing Abilities (11-18)*. London: Macmillan Education Press, 1975.

12. Britton, James. "Research Currents: Second Thoughts on Learning." *Language Arts* 62 (1985): 72-77.

13. Bronowski, Jacob. *The Origins of Knowledge znd Imagination*. New Haven: Yale University Press, 1978.

14. Carlisle, E. Fred. "Teaching Writing Humanistically: From Theory to Action." *English Journal* 67 (April 1978): 35-39.

15. Carter, Jack. "The Human Sciences Program and the Future." *American Biology Teacher* 44 (October 1982): 427-28.

16. Connors, R. J. "Composition Studies and Science." *College English* 45 (January 1983): 1-20.

17. Corbett, Edward P. J. "A Collegiate Writing Program for the '80s." *ADE Bulletin* 78 (July 1984): 108-19.

18. Craig, Betty Jean. "An Alternative to the Current Research Model of Literature." *ADFL Bulletin* 16 (September 1984): 27-30.

19. DeBruin, Jerome, and Gibney, Thomas C. "If You Teach Science and Mathematics, Then Write." *School Science and Mathematics* 84 (January 1984): 33-42.

20. Dick, John A. R., and Esch, Robert M. "Dialogues Among Disciplines: A Plan for Faculty Discussions of Writing Across the Curriculum." *College Composition and Communication* 36 (May 1985): 178-82.

21. Dixon, John. *Growth Through English*. London: National Association for the Teaching of English, 1975.

22. Dobrin, David. "Is Teaching Technical Writing Particularly Objective?" *College English* 47 (March 1985): 237-51.

23. Donlan, Dan. "Teaching Writing in the Content Areas." *Research in the Teaching of English* 8 (1974): 250-62.

24. Douglas, Wallace. *An Introduction to Some Basic Processes in Composition*. Evanston, Ill.: Northwestern University Curriculum Center in English, 1963.

25. Eblen, Charlene. "Writing Across the Curriculum: A Survey of Faculty Views and Classroom Practices." *Research in the Teaching of English* 17 (December 1983): 343-48.

26. Elbow, Peter. *Writing with Power*. New York: Oxford University Press, 1974.

27. Ellman, Neil. "The Two Cultures: Bridging the Gap." *English Journal* 66 (October 1976): 55-56.

28. Emig, Janet. "Inquiry Paradigms and Writing." *College English* 33 (February 1982): 64-75.

29. _____. "Writing as a Mode of Learning." *College Composition and Communication* 28 (May 1977): 123-24.

30. Enke, C. G. "Scientific Writing: One Scientist's Perspective." *English Journal* 67 (April 1978): 40-43.

31. Erickson, Lawrence. "Stop Shouting: Using Writing to Keep Group Decisions on Target." *Executive Educator* 5 (October 1983): 34-35, 37.

32. Estus, Charles. "An Interdisciplinary Approach to Community Studies." *History Teacher* 13 (November 1979): 37–48.

33. Faigley, Lester, and Hanson, Kristine. "Learning to Write in the Social Sciences." *College Composition and Communication* 36 (May 1985): 140–49.

34. Flower, Linda. "The Cognition of Discovery." *College English* 41 (September 1979): 19–37.

35. Fregley, M. S., and Detweiler, J. S. "Teach Them to Think Before They Write." *Journalism Educator* 38 (Spring 1983): 32–35.

36. Fulwiler, Toby. "Journals Across the Disciplines." *English Journal* 69 (December 1980): 14–19.

37. ———. "Showing, Not Telling, at a Faculty Workshop." *College English* 43 (January 1981): 55–63.

38. Gebbard, Ann. "Teaching Writing in Reading and Content Areas." *Journal of Reading* (December 1983): 207–11.

39. Goldberg, D. "Integrating Writing into the Mathematics Curriculum." *Two-Year College Mathematics Journal* 14 (November 1983): 421–24.

40. Gonzalez, Roseann Duenas. "Teaching Mexican-American Students to Write: Capitalizing on the Culture." *English Journal* 71 (November 1982): 20–24.

41. Gopen, George C. "Rhyme and Reason: Why the Study of Poetry Is the Best Preparation for the Study of Law." *College English* 46 (April 1984): 333–47.

42. Greco, J. "Teaching Intermediate Micro-economics by Adopting a Writing Strategy." *Journal of Business Education* 59 (March 1984): 254–56.

43. Griffin, C. W. "Using Writing to Teach Many Disciplines." *Improving College and University Teaching* 31 (Summer 1983): 212–28.

44. Hairston, Maxine. "The Winds of Change: Thomas Kuhn and the Revolution in the Teaching of Writing." *College Composition and Communication* 33 (February 1982): 76–87.

45. Hamilton, David. "Interdisciplinary Writing." *College English* 41 (March 1980): 780–96.

46. Hanf-Buckley, Marilyn. "Mapping: A Technique for Translating Reading into Thinking." *Journal of Reading* (January 1971): 225–30, 270.

47. Harris, Kathryn. "Professional and Technical Writing in the Liberal Arts College." *Improving College and University Teaching* 31 (Summer 1983): 212–28.

48. Henschen, Beth, and Sidlow, Edward. "Undergraduate Student Writing: Possibilities and Benefits of a Group Approach." *Journal of General Education* 35 (1983): 53–63.

49. Hoffman, Eleanor. "Writing for the Social Sciences." *College Composition and Communication* (May 1977): 195–97.

50. Hofstein, Ari, and Yager, Robert E. "Science Education Attuned to Social Issues: Challenges for the '80s." *Science Teacher* 48 (December 1981): 12–14.

51. House, Ken. "Improving Student Writing in Biology." *Biology Teacher* 45 (Summer 1983): 267–70.

52. Jensen, Marvin D. "Memoirs and Journals as Maps of Interpersonal Communication." *Communication Education* 33 (July 1984): 237–42.

53. Johnson, Marvin. "Writing in a Mathematics Class: A Valuable Tool for Learning." *Mathematics Teacher* 76 (February 1983): 117–19.

54. Judy, Stephen. *The ABCs of Literacy.* New York: Oxford University Press, 1980.

55. _____. "Composition and Rhetoric in American Secondary Schools, 1840–1900." *English Journal* 68 (April 1979): 34–39.

56. _____. *The Creative Word.* New York: Random House, 1974.

57. Kirkpatrick, Larry, and Pittendrigh, Adele. "A Writing Teacher in a Physics Classroom." *Physics Teacher* 22 (March 1984): 59–64.

58. Kitzhaber, Albert. "Rhetoric in American Colleges, 1850–1900." Doctoral dissertation, University of Washington, 1953.

59. Klinger, G. A. "Campus Views of College Writing." *College Composition and Communication* 28 (1977): 343–47.

60. Knolblauch, C. H., and Brannon, L. "Writing as Learning Through the Curriculum." *College English* 45 (September 1983): 465–74.

61. Koeller, Shirley. "Expository Writing: A Vital Skill in Science." *Science and Children* (September 1982): 12–15.

62. Kuhn, Thomas. *The Structure of Scientific Revolutions.* Chicago: University of Chicago Press, 1970.

63. Lauer, Janice. "Writing as Inquiry: Some Questions for Teachers." *College English* 33 (February 1982): 89-93.

64. Lewis, William. "Two Technical Writing Assignments." *English Journal* 67 (April 1978): 65-68.

65. Magistrate, Tony. "Measuring Reality: Critical Writing and Television Analysis." *Exercise Exchange* 30 (Fall 1984): 20-21.

66. Marcus, Stephen. "Any Teacher a Writing Teacher?" *Improving College and University Teaching* 28 (Winter 1980): 10-12.

67. _____. "Not Seeing Is Relieving: Invisible Writing with Computers." *Educational Technology* 23 (April 1983): 12-15.

68. Marling, William. "Grading Essays on a Microcomputer." *College English* 46 (1984): 797-810.

69. McCleary, William. "A Case Approach for Teaching Academic Writing." *College Composition and Communication* 36 (May 1985): 203-12

70. Metcalf, James. "Teaching Writing in Physical Education and Recreation." *Journal of Physical Education and Recreation* 50 (November-December 1979): 38.

71. Miller, Carolyn. "A Humanistic Rationale for Teaching Technical Writing." *College English* 40 (February 1979): 610-17.

72. National Education Association. *Report of the Committee on Secondary School Studies*. Washington, D.C.: Government Printing Office, 1893.

73. Newell, George. "Learning from Writing in Two Content Areas." *Research in the Teaching of English* 18 (October 1984): 265-87.

74. *Newsweek*, December 8, 1975.

75. Odell, Lee. "The Process of Writing and the Process of Learning." *College Composition and Communication* 31 (February 1980): 42-50.

76. Palmer, S. E. "How to Help Students with Their Writing." *Chronicle of Higher Education* 26 (July 20, 1983): 11-12

77. Pattison, Robert. "Literacy—Confessions of a Heretic." In *Language, Schooling, and Society*, edited by Stephen Tchudi. Montclair, N.J.: Boynton Cook, 1985.

78. Pearce, D. L. "Guidelines for the Use and Evaluation of Writing in Content Classrooms." *Journal of Reading* 27 (December 1983): 212-18.

PE 1001
. C6

79. Piaget, Jean. *The Language and Thought of the Child.* New York: New American Library, 1957.

80. Polanyi, Michael. *Personal Knowledge.* Chicago: University of Chicago Press, 1962.

81. Raimes, Ann. "Writing and Learning Across the Curriculum: The Experience of a Faculty Seminar." *College English* 41 (March 1980): 797–813.

82. Rizzolo, Patricia. "Peer Tutors Make Good Teachers." *Improving College and University Teaching* 30 (Summer 1982): 115–19.

83. Rose, Mike. "When Faculty Talk About Writing." *College English* 41 (November 1979): 272–79.

84. Ross, Fred, and Jarosz, Mitchell. "Integrating Science Writing: A Biology and English Teacher Get Together." *English Journal* 67 (April 1978): 51–55.

85. Rubin, Donalee. "Evaluating Freshman Writers: What Do Students Really Learn?" *College English* 45 (April 1983): 373–79.

86. Scheffler, Judith. "Composition with Content: An Interdisciplinary Approach." *College Composition and Communication* 20, no. 1 (1979): 51–56.

87. Schwartz, Mimi. "Response to Writing: A College-Wide Perspective." *College English* 46 (January 1984): 55–62.

88. Shuman, R. Baird. "School-Wide Writing Instruction." *English Journal* 74 (1984): 54–57.

89. Spack, Ruth, and Sadow, Catherine. "Student Writing in Journals in ESL Freshman Composition." *TESOL Quarterly* 17 (December 1983): 575–93.

90. Stevenson, John W. "Writing as a Liberal Art." *Liberal Education* 70 (Spring 1984): 57–62.

91. Tabor, Kenneth. "Gaining Successful Writing in the Foreign Language Classroom." *Foreign Language Annals* 17 (April 1984): 123–24.

92. Tchudi, Susan, and Tchudi, Stephen. *The Young Writer's Handbook.* New York: Charles Scribner's Sons, 1984.

93. Troutman, Benjamin, and others. "Interdisciplinary English: Methods and Materials." *English Journal* 66 (October 1976): 49–54.

94. Troyka, Lynn, and Nudelman, Jerrold. *Taking Action: Writing, Reading, Speaking and Listening Through Simulation Games.* Englewood Cliffs, N. J.: Prentice-Hall, 1975.

95. University of North Carolina, Wilmington. *Writing Across the UNCW Campus.* Wilmington, N.C.: UNCW, n.d.

96. Van Nostrand, A. D. "Writing and the Generation of Knowledge." *Social Education* 43 (1979): 178-80.

97. Veit, Richard. "De-Grading Composition: Do Papers Need Grades?" *College English* 41 (December 1979): 423-35.

98. Ventre, Raymond. "Developing Writing: Social Studies Assignments." *Social Education* 43 (1979): 181-83, 197.

99. Vygotsky, L. S. *Thought and Language.* Cambridge: MIT Press, 1961.

100. Wartell, Michael. "Science and the Liberal Arts." *Liberal Education* 70 (Spring 1979): 21-25.

101. Weeks, Ruth Mary. *A Correlated Curriculum.* New York: D. Appleton, 1936.

102. Weiss, Robert, and Peich, Michael. "Faculty Attitude Change in a Cross-Disciplinary Writing Workshop." *College Composition and Communication* 31 (February 1980): 33-41.

103. Wilkes, John. "Science Writing: Who? What? How?" *English Journal* 67 (April 1978): 56-60.

104. Wolfe, Denny. "Opting for Newthink: Interdisciplinary English in the Decades Ahead." *English Journal* 74 (October 1984): 28-31.

105. Yates, Joanne M. *Research Implications for Writing in the Content Areas.* Washington, D.C.: National Education Association, 1983.

106. Zemelman, Steven. "How College Teachers Encourage Student Writing." *Research in the Teaching of English* 11 (1977): 227-34.